Praise for **Gerard Straub**

Gerard Straub's first book of poetic reflections, *Thoughts of a Blind Beggar,* was published in 2007. *A Journey to Meekness* is a new collection of his poetic prayers and reflections.

"Gerry Straub underwent a spectacular conversion, from success as an atheistic Hollywood TV producer into the downwardly mobile world of St. Francis and Christian discipleship. Now a groundbreaking documentary filmmaker on behalf of the world's poorest, Straub shares with us the contemplative side of that Gospel journey. Like the writings of Thomas Merton, Carlo Carretto, and Henri Nouwen, *Thoughts of a Blind Beggar* needs to be kept close by for early morning or late-night meditation. It stirs up new insights into our own poverty, our own need for prayer, vision, and God's healing touch, and pushes us forward on our own journey to God."

—Fr. John Dear, Author of *Living Peace, Transfiguration*
and *The Questions of Jesus*

"Gerard Straub's transparency will bring our affluent and insulated hearts to their knees. *Thoughts of a Blind Beggar* provokes prayer and instigates action to repair our world's brokenness. A profoundly simple but dangerously honest book destined to change lives."

—Jonathan Montaldo, The Merton Institute
for Contemplative Living

"Open this book to any page, and you will find the wisdom of one who has been illuminated by his care and love for the poor and the marginal. Straub is a blind man who sees with the eyes of the Christ he has seen in other human beings."

—Murray Bodo, OFM, Author of *A Journey and a Dream*

Praise for
The Loneliness and Longing of Saint Francis

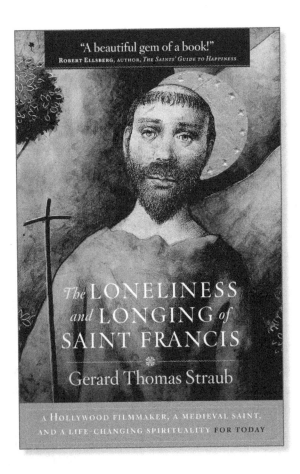

"A beautiful gem of a book!"
ROBERT ELLSBERG, AUTHOR, *THE SAINTS' GUIDE TO HAPPINESS*

The LONELINESS
and LONGING *of*
SAINT FRANCIS

Gerard Thomas Straub

A HOLLYWOOD FILMMAKER, A MEDIEVAL SAINT,
AND A LIFE-CHANGING SPIRITUALITY FOR TODAY

"An atmosphere of prayer pervades Gerard Thomas Straub's prose in his new work on Saint Francis of Assisi. This is an engagingly contemplative book. He interweaves meditations on the inner experiences of his personal biography with the details of the Saint's life. Searching for the meaning of his own life's journey, Straub excavates below Francis' biography for the spirituality that grounded the Saint's encounters with God in all things. The author's history of moving from a pampered life to one that serves communities of the poorest all over the world is an instructive parable for our times. His unromantic reflections on the arduous nature of Francis' self-awakening point toward the difficult way out of self-centered loneliness to a more exacting, but in the end more joyous because self-transcending, way of living. Straub maps a clear path that leads out of isolation to communion with all human beings through confessing our common weaknesses and realizing our inter-dependence. He rekindles a Franciscan source of light for the only realistic way to our becoming a more morally grounded world body of spiritual workers, together creating a culture of prayer that truly longs for God."

—Jonathan Montaldo, editor, *Dialogues with Silence:*
Thomas Merton's Prayers & Drawings

"Distilling his prize-winning, *The Sun and Moon Over Assisi*, and re-fashioning an image of St. Francis drawn from his work and presence among the poorest of the poor in places like Uganda and Haiti, Gerard Straub gives us a St. Francis of and for the Poor: the materially poor and those who are poor in spirit. Here is a humble, mellow pen 'trying to fall in love with Francis again' and in the process finding words to reveal the depths of a St. Francis who speaks to the poverty of our own loneliness and longing in the 21st Century. As in his first book, Straub intertwines his own on-going story with that of St. Francis, revealing what a labor of love is his search for the secret of the peace and joy of St. Francis."

—Murray Bodo, OFM, author of *Francis and Jesus*

"Through his encounter with St. Francis of Assisi, Gerry Straub came to love Christ and the poor. That encounter transformed his life. Here in this beautiful gem of a book he traces the footsteps of St. Francis in his age and our own, showing a way of prayer and compassion with the power to transform our hearts, and thereby transform the world."

—Robert Ellsberg, author of *The Saints' Guide to Happiness*

"Forged in the fiery smithy of the author's own soul, this beautiful book is urgent, passionate and compelling. Its unique power springs from the fusion of Straub's personal involvement in today's most shocking scenes of human poverty, his sense of the extreme, essential soul of St Francis, and his intense awareness of his own vulnerability and demons. In this fire a spiritual masterpiece is born."

—Fr. Daniel O'Leary, author, *Already Within:
Divining the Hidden Spring*

"Many of us speak of biblical paradox. Gerry Straub lives it. Through his art and commitment, we have a deeper understanding of this difficult matter of richness in poverty. He has wrestled with that reality at great length and, through the struggle, gained unique insights into the person of St. Francis."

—Tom Roberts, Editor at large, National Catholic Reporter

"Gerard Thomas Straub has devoted his life to shining the light of the gospel into what Pope Francis has called the "existential peripheries" of our time. Through film, photography, and writing he has highlighted the urgent need for a compassionate response to chronic poverty. I am privileged to call him a friend and brother."

—Fr. Hugh McKenna, OFM, *the Minister Provincial,
Franciscan Friars, Province of Ireland*

"A Franciscan nun once told me that part of her work was to rescue Saint Francis from the birdbaths in which so often he is held captive. Gerry Straub's book does just that, presenting an unperfumed Francis who modeled his life on Christ's in ways that amazed the medieval world into which he was born and that remain startling to the present day. If you are willing to meet a rag-dressed beggar who has changed the world, this book opens the door."

—Jim Forest, author of *All Is Grace: A Biography of Dorothy Day*

"Straub not only knows the life of Saint Francis well but has lived a Franciscan life through his commitment to the poor. This is a book that rings with authenticity. Highly recommended."

—Lawrence S. Cunningham, author of *Things Seen and Unseen*

"In this bold tale, author Gerry Straub puts his finger on the desire that is within us all to live simply and sustainably, with holy wisdom and a strong sense of the beauty around us. Bringing together his own journey with that of St Francis of Assisi, he provides a common, universal language that helps us all see the Creator with new eyes."

—Bill Huebsch, author of *The Joy of the Gospel Group Reading Guide*

"There are stories that will always be told again and again. The story of Brother Francis, the saint of Assisi, is one of those. And every time Francis' story is told, a personal touch is added. This is exactly what Gerard Straub does. Taking us through the stages of Francis' life, from his youth to his death, he makes connections with contemporary events and with his own life. "St. Francis of Brooklyn" (p. 231ss.) is a good illustration of the originality of this book."

—Jean-François Godet-Calogeras, *Professor of Franciscan Studies at St. Bonaventure University.*

A Journey to Meekness

PRAYER POEMS & REFLECTIONS

Gerard Thomas Straub, OFS

Pax et Bonum
COMMUNICATIONS

Published by:
Pax et Bonum Communications
FT. PIERCE, FL

Copyright © 2022 Gerard Straub

ISBN-13: 979-8-9860888-0-8

Editorial consultation
Joe Heil

Cover and interior
Gary A. Rosenberg • www.thebookcouple.com

Printed in the United States of America

"If we could but find a rhythm of being which could balance a contemplative grace, a poetry of motion and an accompanying stillness and silence, our pilgrimage through this world would flow in beauty through the most ragged and forsaken heartlands of confusion and dishevelment."

—JOHN O'DONOHUE

Contents

PROLOGUE
An Island of Hope in a Sea of Despair   xiii

PREFACE
We Are All Fragments   xxv

INTRODUCTION
Prayer by Prayer   1

PART ONE
Prayer Poems   3

PART TWO
Poetic Reflections   29

PART THREE
The Fragrant Spirit of Life   143

PART FOUR
The Sun & Moon Over Assisi   163

PART FIVE
The Perfection of Love   187

PART SIX
Thoughts of a Blind Beggar   205

PART SEVEN
Endless Exodus   237

EPILOGUE
Closing Prayers   271

ABOUT THE AUTHOR
Gerry on Gerry   275

PROLOGUE

An Island of Hope in a Sea of Despair

by Joseph Lewis Heil

This essay was originally published in the Spring 2022 edition of Notre Dame Magazine. *Joseph Lewis Heil is a subscriber to Gerry Straub's daily Journal from Haiti. His brother, John Heil, is a member of Santa Chiara Children's Center's board of directors. Joe's essay was based on material in Gerry's Journal and from a number of books Gerry has written. Straub had no idea Joe was writing the essay. The editors at* Notre Dame Magazine *loved the piece and elected to publish it. In the same edition of the magazine, an essay about Vincent van Gogh, written by Gerry Straub, was also published.*

Moïse Straub, two weeks old, arrived at the front gate of Santa Chiara Children's Center in Port-au-Prince, Haiti, on the Ides of March, 2021. He was cradled in the arms of a woman who was not his mother. The real mother, after giving birth in the notorious slum of Cité Soleil, gave Moïse, Haitian Creole for Moses, to a stranger. Blood and fluid still covered the newborn. The distressed, teenage mother had begged the woman to tend the infant until she returned. She never did.

There was some reluctance among Santa Chiara's staff to accept the child. Nevertheless, the founder, Gerard Thomas Straub, decided to keep the baby boy, even though Santa Chiara's primary mission is caring for and educating girls. To turn Moïse away would send him to certain death in one of the world's most impoverished, dangerous, filthy and degrading slums. Straub named the child, giving him his own surname and filing to adopt him. Moïse thus joined five other abandoned children also named Straub. The odyssey of how Gerry Straub, 74, came to run a home for abandoned

Haitian kids and become an adoptive father began many years ago under the bright, television-studio lights of New York City and Hollywood.

Straub grew up in a devout Catholic family in a middle-class neighborhood of Queens. His parents made daily Mass and the rosary hallmarks of family life. Straub attended Catholic grade school and served as an altar boy. A cousin was a Redemptorist missionary priest. Catholicism became an essential element within Straub's young, sensitive mind.

At 13, he entered a Vincentian minor seminary in Princeton, New Jersey. He lasted two semesters. His dream of going to China as a missionary, he has said, "died at the hands of doubt." The bigotry he had observed in his quiet Queens neighborhood as it progressed toward racial integration made him wonder why he should go to China to save souls when people on his own block seemed unchanged by Christian teaching.

After graduating from St. John's Prep in 1964, the year the Beatles invaded America, Straub landed a four-week summer job at CBS in New York. His task was to answer mail-in ticket requests for the Beatles' appearance on an upcoming *Ed Sullivan Show*. He completed the job in two weeks and spent the next two weeks "walking the corridors, poking my head into studios, marveling at the cameras, lights and sets," he remembers. "It was a magical world that captivated my imagination." Such tireless, teenage nosiness was readily noticed.

CBS offered Straub a clerical job and, to his parents' horror, he took it, rather than going to college. Soon he was selected for an executive training program that placed him in a new job every three months. He accrued knowledge of the business so rapidly that at 21 he was made a full-time executive. Television became his life.

He worked at CBS until 1978. Several years later at ABC, he became an associate producer of the persistently popular, long-running soap opera, *General Hospital*. He worked with Elizabeth Taylor, Demi Moore, Tony Randall and others. At NBC he was the executive producer of another soap, *The Doctors*, that featured a young Alec Baldwin. One day, alone in his office watching his own show, he wondered, *Who would watch this garbage?* Straub was commercially successful, well paid, but deeply unfulfilled.

In 1987, approaching his 40th birthday, he produced his last soap. He wanted to channel his creativity into literary fiction, so he retreated to upstate New York, reading works of philosophy and theology. In spite of those influences, he wrote two books mildly in support of atheism, one of which was a dark novel about a man so exhausted in his search for God that he committed suicide. Straub describes the book as an angry scream at the Catholic Church. It did not sell.

The second novel was about a writer obsessed with the disparate lives of Vincent van Gogh and St. Francis of Assisi. After two more years of writing and feeling stuck, Straub decided to visit Arles in the south of France, where van Gogh had spent some of his most prolific years. He also decided to visit Assisi in Italy in hopes that the spirit of the two men, still alive in those distant towns, would inspire him to complete his book.

During his many years away from God and the Church, Straub had remained friends with a Franciscan friar who kindly tolerated his unbelief. He now asked him for help finding accommodations in Rome. That's how, in March 1995, Straub arrived at the gate of the friary at Collegio Sant' Isidoro, a 400-year-old seminary run by Irish Franciscans. He was led to a small, austere room and told he was welcome to join the friars for dinner. The days were his to wander the busy, noisy, fascinating streets of Rome on his own.

After unpacking and heading out with an explorer's enthusiasm, Straub passed an open door to Sant' Isidoro's church. A beautiful statue caught his eye. He entered, but not to pray. He looked around, admired the architecture, then decided to sit and rest for a moment in the quiet, peaceful, darkened nave.

"This empty church and an empty man met in a moment of grace," he recalls in *The Sunrise of the Soul*, a spiritual memoir. As he rested in the silence "something highly unexpected" happened: "God broke through the silence. And everything changed. In the womb of the dark church, I picked up a copy of the Liturgy of the Hours and opened it randomly to Psalm 63. In boldface above the psalm it said, 'A soul thirsting for God.' As I read the words of the psalm my soul leapt with joy: 'God, you are my God, I am seeking you, my soul is thirsting for you, my flesh is longing for you....'

"Without warning, I felt the overwhelming presence of God," he continues. "I felt immersed in a sea of love. I knew ... that God was real, that God loved me, that the hunger and thirst I had felt for so long could only be satisfied by God. In that moment of revelation, I was transformed from an atheist into a pilgrim."

At Sant' Isidoro he attended morning and evening prayer and daily Mass. He hadn't been part of the Church for over 15 years, nor had he received the Blessed Sacrament. One evening the guardian friar asked Straub if he'd like to talk for a while. That simple, gracious invitation commenced a three-hour conversation culminating in the sacrament of Reconciliation. Straub felt intensely liberated. The next day he received the Eucharist. From that moment, he adopted St. Francis as his spiritual guide. Over the years, Assisi would become his spiritual home.

Another friar introduced him to a Jesuit priest, head of the communications department at the Pontifical Gregorian University. Quite unexpectedly, he was asked to talk to a class and give students the chance to question a former Hollywood producer. That led to an invitation to teach a two-week course on creative writing for film and television in September 1995.

During his first fall of teaching, Straub met Father John Navone, a Jesuit professor of theology at the university and literary figure of some note. Straub told him about his van Gogh-St. Francis novel, and the priest offered to read it.

That December, Straub received a 10-page letter in which the priest, "cut my novel to pieces . . . bluntly telling me how the novel did not work on any level."

But there was more. On the last page, Navone wrote, "the writing on St. Francis is the best I have ever read. Throw this book out and write a book about St. Francis."

Straub took that advice and spent four years writing about the saint he loved, hoping to come to understand Francis's love not only for the poor, but for poverty itself. Voluntary poverty was for St. Francis a way to be utterly dependent upon God for everything. A pragmatic man, Straub found that concept difficult to grasp, especially within the materialistic culture from which he came.

And yet for all Straub's difficulties in trying to understand the saint, the Catholic Press Association in 2001 named his book, *The Sun & Moon Over Assisi*, the best spirituality hardcover book of the year.

Hoping to gain a deeper understanding of St. Francis's love for poverty, Straub lived for a month with Franciscan friars who served the homeless at St. Francis Inn in Philadelphia. The experience was transformational.

Every conception he had about homeless and addicted persons was wrong. He found instead they were real people, people he had callously and shamefully dismissed as worthless. The friars who dedicated their lives to serving the poor inspired him to make a film about St. Francis Inn. With the help of a friend from *Good Morning America,* he assembled a crew and shot the film in only four days. Incredibly, that humble effort, *We Have a Table for Four Ready,* was picked up by PBS and broadcast at Thanksgiving time for many years.

The friars of the inn have received thousands of dollars in donations from viewers of the film. They have a waiting list of volunteers. Donated funds expanded the kitchen and added a second-floor chapel. Every day about 60 people, many recovering from addiction, attend Mass at the inn.

The film's impact revealed a new purpose for Straub's life. He felt impelled to "put the power of film at the service of the poor."

In Rome, the head of the Order of Friars Minor, who had read and liked *The Sun & Moon Over Assisi,* summoned Straub for a visit. Straub expressed how he was still struggling with the meaning of poverty in his life. He then asked permission to live somewhere, anywhere, with friars as they served the poor. Three weeks later he landed in Kolkata, India. With him he carried an idea and several cameras. Over the next 15 months he visited 39 cities in 11 nations. He filmed and photographed the most horrific slums in India, Kenya, Brazil, Jamaica, the Philippines and Mexico. The products of all that travel, hardship and work would be a photo book, a short film narrated by Martin Sheen, and the affliction of post-traumatic stress disorder.

Scenes of suffering in a slum would flash across Straub's mind, causing him to weep. He had taken thousands of vivid, pain-filled photographs trying to understand the cruelty and senselessness of poverty that was killing millions around the world, including countless children who were dying from malnutrition and curable diseases. Filming people who were living and dying in filth and squalor filled him with an unshakeable sadness. He wrote about those "lost and forgotten, their desperate lives not important enough or worthy enough to save. They were disposable people."

He spent hours studying and selecting photographs to include in his photo book, *When Did I See You Hungry?,* published in 2002. The task became a nonstop horror show running wildly in his mind. And yet, when it was completed and as the years went by, he continued filming and photographing in Uganda, Kenya, Brazil, Peru, Honduras, El Salvador and Haiti. Everywhere he went deepened in his mind, heart and soul the harsh reality of the unjust, unwarranted, unnecessary suffering caused by the affluent world's unwillingness to unselfishly share and care for these least of our brothers and sisters, all beloved children of God. For Straub, not helping those in need became the greatest sin of a heartless humanity.

Today, in addition to having made two dozen documentary films on global poverty, Straub has published seven books and documented homelessness in Los Angeles, Detroit, Philadelphia and Budapest, Hungary. Since 2002, he has given over 250 presentations at churches, high schools and colleges across the United States, Canada, France, Italy and Hungary. His work has earned him honorary doctoral degrees from three Catholic universities. He has lectured and shown his films at many Catholic universities, including Notre Dame in 2002 and '04.

Was it destiny that placed Straub in Port-au-Prince in December 2009? He had gone there to do what he had done in so many other cities. His first visit to Cité Soleil—City of the Sun—would prove haunting: a decrepit landscape of tin shacks, tarpaper roofs, rotting garbage and open sewers. He saw a little girl urinating on a heap of trash, a woman openly defecating, naked children with bloated bellies running barefoot through pig-infested mud. The putrid, nauseating stench was intensified by the unrelenting sun. It was almost too much for this sensitive man, so deeply afflicted by years of bearing witness to the world's worst poverty. It left him feeling helpless and devastated. He retreated to his home in Burbank, California, for Christmas and New Year's, but celebrated nothing.

Then on January 12, 2010, miles beneath the rough roads of Port-au-Prince and the nearby city of Léogâne, a contractional deformation along a fault line generated a large-scale earthquake. Poorly constructed concrete and masonry buildings collapsed, killing more than 200,000 people and leaving more than 1 million without shelter.

A week later, Straub was invited to accompany a medical team flying from Dallas to Port-au-Prince on a plane crammed with medicine and equipment. He was to film their relief efforts. With less than three hours' notice, he joined the 22-member team to load the 737, filling the cargo hold and every unoccupied seat with supplies.

When the plane landed in the destroyed city, Straub felt he had entered an inferno of suffering and despair from which few would escape. The choking odor of dead bodies entombed in flattened buildings sickened him. Streets strewn with mangled or burned corpses horrified him. Seeing a young boy's decaying foot stick out from the rubble of his ruined school and the skeletal remains of a person burned to death, charred his mind and memory. Amputations were performed without anesthesia. It was more than Straub could bear. He wept, not fully realizing that his life was being changed far more radically than when he had left the hollow glamour of Hollywood more than two decades before.

He again developed PTSD. He knew he had to stop filming the poor. It was not enough. In the spirit of St. Francis, he knew he needed somehow to serve the poor, walk with them, live with them, become poor with them.

By 2015, Straub was living in a deeply impoverished section of Port-au-Prince. He heard gunfire almost every night. In the beginning, he simply intended to provide daycare for the children of poor women who earned very little selling homemade goods on streets too dangerous for kids. As in so many other cities of the world, children would be dropped off at the daycare in the early morning and picked up in the early evening. But Port-au-Prince is no ordinary city. Straub learned of one street-vending mother who sold homemade pasta. A man demanded a free bowl. She refused. He shot and killed her little boy who was seated on the ground beside her.

To help prevent such incomprehensible tragedies, Straub planned to shelter, feed and entertain such kids, keeping them safe and busy until their mothers returned to take them home, a home that was probably a mere shack with no running water or electricity. But within a month, something happened that Straub had not anticipated: 22 children were living and sleeping at the daycare. Their mothers had dropped them off but never returned to pick them up. He would learn this was not unusual. A hospital where he had taken kids for treatment asked him to take in children who had been abandoned there. Even Mother Teresa's Missionaries of Charity asked Straub to welcome unwanted kids left at their gate.

Within two years, 72 youngsters of varying ages were living with Straub and his growing staff. An infant was brought to him at two days old. His distraught mother had left him on a garbage dump to perish amid the filth and rats. Straub well understood that the daycare by necessity had evolved into a refuge and orphanage for homeless and parentless children, especially for girls, who are most vulnerable. He knew the daycare had to become a home. He made it one.

Straub named his center in honor of Santa Chiara, St. Clare of Assisi, who was St. Francis's most faithful follower. By selecting that name, he wished to impart a Franciscan spirit to the home. Santa Chiara is unlike traditional orphanages. It's more akin to a field hospital for kids, many of whom come to Straub seriously ill and often severely malnourished. Santa Chiara is essentially a sanctuary. Initially the motto was "A Place for Kids to Be Kids." In time, as the daycare transitioned into an orphanage, it became "A Home of Hope and Healing for Kids."

The unwanted, unwashed, homeless, abused and abandoned children of Cité Soleil are on a tortured exodus to nowhere. For them there is no promise, no hope and no future. They live within an abyss of despair. Yet among them Straub found his authentic life and learned the true meaning of sacrificial love. Santa Chiara is a place where some of the children of Cité Soleil get a chance to be safe, to grow and to learn.

Presently, Santa Chiara is housed in its third building, which provides comfort, cleanliness and physical safety. Many of the children have been there for six years, right from the start. They know nothing of the violence and mayhem that often occurs outside the walls of their home. The Missionaries of Charity often visit, as does a Passionist priest from Mexico and several of Straub's priest-friends from the U.S. Everyone marvels that Santa Chiara, in the words of one visitor, is the "happiest orphanage" they have ever seen in Haiti. The sincere love among the staff and children reflects brightly in their eyes.

In the last several years, the number of children living at the center has gradually reduced. Some were moved to orphanages that could better meet their needs. Others returned to their families in cases where the parent or parents were again able to care for them. Family reunification, though rare, is always a priority.

Thirty-six Santa Chiara children attend an excellent private school. The center has a fine medical clinic staffed by two part-time nurses, one assistant nurse and two part-time doctors. One doctor is a highly regarded pediatrician at a nearby children's hospital. The other lives in the neighborhood. In addition to her normal hours at Santa Chiara, she is called upon for emergencies—Straub himself once needed five stitches in his head after a nasty fall. With more than a dozen kids in diapers, the clinic has been an invaluable part of the center's success. Tragically, in Haiti, many poor children never reach their 5th birthday.

In the last two years, many charitable organizations have fled Haiti. In March 2020, when the coronavirus became a pandemic, the Haitian government banned all incoming visitors from the U.S. For a week, empty commercial planes landed in Port-au-Prince to fetch Americans home. Family and friends urged Straub to leave. But he knew if he left, he would not be able to return to his kids for a long time. That was unacceptable, so he chose to stay.

Two months later, he was struck with COVID-19. The Missionaries of Charity obtained oxygen tanks that kept him alive for seven critical days. The superior was so sure Straub would die that she sought a priest to administer last rites. After he recovered, he developed a boil from a MRSA infection. It had to be lanced at a hospital that had no Novocain. Two attendants and a priest held Straub down. He screamed throughout the torturous procedure.

Because of Haiti's deteriorating social, economic and political conditions, including the assassination of an unpopular president, the past few years have seen escalating civil unrest and gang violence. Initially, gangs disrupted traffic by setting up strategic roadblocks of burning tires, their black smoke fouling the already polluted Caribbean air. Then they began burning supermarkets and pharmacies. Straub's life was threatened when he and an 8-year-old girl were driving home after attending Mass at the Missionaries of Charity chapel. They were surrounded by a gang holding gasoline cans above the car and threatening to set it ablaze. He pleaded with the gang leader to let the girl go, let her live. Mercifully, the man let both of them go.

By early 2021, people were killed or kidnapped on a daily basis. Straub had to travel with an armed guard. Then, in May and June, a lull in the kidnapping occurred, but word on the street was that it would soon start again. Seventeen members of the U.S.-based Christian Aid Ministries were kidnapped in October; by December all were released or had escaped. Father Tom Hagen, a friend of Straub's who has ministered for 30 years in the slums of Cité Soleil, has said that "no one in the States can ever understand the reality of Haiti."

Straub often wonders why, in his near-old age, he's in Haiti running a "happy orphanage." By his own admission, in a professional sense, he really doesn't know how to run an orphanage. Drawn to the solitude of monasticism and the contemplative life, he lives in a crowded slum where screaming kids, crying babies and gunfire are the soundtrack of his daily life. Every day in Port-au-Prince the potential for deadly harm persists. Nevertheless, he remains in Haiti saving the lives of precious, innocent children dealt a very bad hand, kids who matter little to few outside the staff and supporters of Santa Chiara. He's rooted in Haiti because he cannot and will not abandon them. His devotion defines the truest meaning of sacrificial love.

Straub writes, "The slums of Haiti exist because we as the human family have forgotten God and turned our backs on God's children." Difficult words to be sure. But Gerry Straub has the right to say them—to shout them—because he has turned with open arms and heart to the least of God's unwanted, unloved little ones.

A graduate of the Notre Dame's Program of Liberal Studies, Joseph Lewis Heil is the author of two novels, The War Less Civil *and* Judas in Jerusalem. *He resides in suburban Milwaukee.*

For information about the Santa Chiara Children's Center in Haiti, please visit our website: www.SantaChiaraCC.org

The proceeds of this book will be donated to the home for abandoned children.

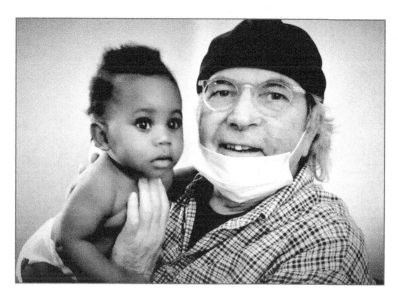

Moïse Straub and Gerry Staub (November 10, 2021)

Some of the children at Santa Chiara. (January 22, 2022)

PREFACE

We Are All Fragments

This book is filled with sentences (hopefully) and not mere fragments. A fragment is a part of something that has broken away from the whole. It is detached, isolated, an incomplete part of something larger. In a literary sense, a fragment is part of a work that remains or was left unfinished. The fragments in this book, while consisting of complete sentences, are in fact detached particles of a larger truth that will always remain unknown.

We are all fragments, part of the fullness of God, thousands of little bits of colored tile in the vast mosaic that is the Divine face, each of us a tiny part of the infinite reality that is the face of God. As the great 15th century German mystic Nicholas of Cusa said, "Every face you encounter in life is a face of the Faceless One." The face of God is so vast it is faceless from our limited perspective.

The "fragments" gathered together here are little bits of truth that are part of a far greater, far larger, far wiser truth that we must all journey toward. I like the metaphor of a road, that we are on a journey to our real home, a home in a faraway place that will cloak us in love and mercy, kindness and forgiveness, and allow us to heal our fragmentary selves and allow us to blend into the safety and unity a truly Holy Family, where God our Mother and Father watches over us, protects us, nourishes us and loves us into and through all eternity.

Each morning we are awakened to the presence of God. When our hearts and minds are awakened by God, each morning becomes a silent symphony, each day is orchestrated according to the ways of harmony and peace and each moment becomes a sacramental moment where heaven and earth have the potential to meet. Our journey to God begins afresh each morning. If we begin the day in prayer, in God, then the day will flow out from God and lead us home to God. Let us pray.

St. Francis understood we all are the human face of Jesus; he knew that all of humanity comprises the divine face. God assumed flesh and was born into a world of oppression and persecution. Can we ever grasp the reality of the divine presence dwelling in a depraved humanity and that subsequently every man, woman and child is uniquely precious, equal and blessed, all brothers and sisters?

The old material so touched me in a fresh, unexpected way that I was inspired to pen new reflections for a reincarnated, all-poetic form version of *Fragments*. Throughout this new work that is focused on mysticism and mercy, three themes emerged: stillness, silence, and service. Before getting to the reflections, I want to offer a gentle suggestion on how best to read this book with a listening ear.

In a world where we are surrounded by a cacophony of sound and noise, it is hard to absorb and practice St. Benedict's dictum to his monks that they "listen" to the word of God through the printed text of Sacred Scriptures. Unlike the early cave dwelling followers of St. Benedict in the mountains of Norcia in the southeastern part of Umbria in Italy, we have a boisterous cocktail party going on inside our heads. I'm often astounded by how a wonderfully beautiful thought I have can be quickly snuffed out by an ugly, mean-spirited, spiteful thought.

Modern day Benedictine monks teach a new way of learning to read prayerfully but to do so with a heart and mind open to God, which is called *Lectio Divina*. It is an active kind of reading. We are not just sitting with a book in our hands as a passive consumer. At the same time, we are not hassling God with our own agenda and preoccupations.

In a formal or traditional way, *Lectio Divina* consists of four steps: reading, meditating, praying, and contemplating—*lectio, meditatio, oratio,* and *contemplatio*. That structure, however, sounds like a "how to" formula, and this is not *Lectio Divina's* purpose. Perhaps St. John of the Cross explains it best: "Seek in reading, and you will find in meditation. Knock in prayer, and it will be opened to you in contemplation."

This is all to caution you not read this book straight through as you would with any work of nonfiction, but when a reflection in the book triggers a thought within you, put the book down and follow where the thought leads. When the thoughts fade out, pick up the book and continue reading . . . or go about your day. Occasionally the thought that is triggered while reading is something you're not proud of, and that's OK. Just pray that God guides you to a deeper insight. *Lectio Divina* is an exercise in listening to the heart's murmuring, in learning *how* to listen, and in facing up to all that we want, which we perhaps should not want. True *Lectio Divina* will result in a genuine repentance, a true change in how one lives a spiritual life.

Lectio Divina means "divine reading." This is a way of reading different from the ordinary search in books for facts and entertainment. It is a way of reading geared towards enabling one to discover the heart's deepest reactions and desires. An Orthodox monk and priest who is a friend of mine suggested that:

> Lectio Divina is a reverential listening to what the heart is saying in response to the text. Lectio Divina is not a theological analysis. It is not a confirmation of the creed to which one adheres. It is a way of discovering what the heart wants, what it thinks, especially those realities ordinarily hidden from one's conscious awareness. Lectio Divina is, as St. Benedict states, "to listen with the ear of the heart."

If *A Journey to Meekness* is read slowly in that manner, by the end the reader will find that they have come face-to-face with feelings and thoughts within themselves that they had no idea were there. In that way, this humble book can be a spiritual retreat, leaving the person with new insights for her or his own pilgrimage.

A Note about the Photography

All the photographs in this book were taken by the author in India, Uganda, Haiti, Turkey, The Philippines, and Italy.

INTRODUCTION
Prayer by Prayer

little over 20 years ago, I began praying the Liturgy of the Hours every morning. In doing so I became attracted to a few Psalms that I wanted to have handy for quick access during the day. I simply typed them and parked them in a MS-Word document. One day I came across a prayer written by a 3rd century Orthodox saint that reminded me of my favorite psalm, Psalm 63, and so I added it to the file. This inspired me to pen my own short prayers. Slowly I began to add a number of beautiful and insightful prayers written by saints.

Whenever my spiritual reading came across a quotation on prayer or the inner spiritual life that really spoke to me, I added it to the growing file. The collection was becoming alive. I also began to incorporate my own poetic reflections on spirituality, some of which emerged from a poverty film I was making in some far-off slum in the developing world. Soon I found myself organizing the haphazard collection of psalms, prayers, reflections, and quotations into an order that helped me direct my attention toward God first thing every day. Little by little, psalm by psalm, prayer by prayer, quote by quote, my humble little collection was growing into something I treasured. I found myself opening the file first thing every morning as I sipped my first cup of coffee. I used the collection as a way of entering into my daily morning prayer time, some days only reading a few pages, some days reading all of them and some days just skipping around the collection, perhaps briefly meditating on one entry.

About ten years ago, I posted one of my prayers on my now-defunct blog, and the response really surprised me. I decided to share my then 25-page collection with a few friends. Again, the response was very positive. In the following years it grew to over 130 pages. But in 2015, when I began my ministry to help abandoned kids in Haiti, writing and distributing the collection ended. In the spring of 2021, I stumbled upon the file containing all the prayers, quotes, and reflections and it really touched me. I stripped away all the quotes and focused on the prayer poems and the poetic reflections. I gave the new organized version a name that seemed to fit not only the collection but also my journey for over 20 years: *A Journey to Weakness.*

The first person I shared the revised collection with is a man I deeply respected, though we have never met in person. He was a faithful reader of my daily Haiti Journal and often responds to an entry with some very wise words. He liked the collection very much. He offered one impactful comment: "I think a more pertinent title would be *A Journey to Meekness.* Meekness has a more positive connotation than weakness. Jesus was meek and humble of heart, but He was far from weak. We are all essentially weak. Pride can be our downfall. It is wise to strive for (journey to) meekness of heart in imitation of our Lord."

I said *Amen,* and changed the title.

Gerry Straub
March 31, 2022
Port-au-Prince, Haiti

PART ONE

Prayer Poems

"Prayer is the mother and wellspring of the movement in God."

—St. Bonaventure

3

Bless This Time of Prayer

*Unless the prayer which you intend to offer God is important and
meaningful to you first, you will not be able to present it to the
Lord. If you are inattentive to the words you pronounce, if your
heart does not respond to them, or if your life is not turned in the
same direction as your prayer, it will not reach out Godwards.*

—ANTHONY BLOOM, CREATIVE PRAYER: DAILY READINGS
WITH METROPOLITAN ANTHONY OF SOUROZH

O God, this time of prayer
is important to me,
because You are important to me.
I do not want to rush through it,
mindlessly uttering mere words
or, worse, empty words.
Yet, as my Creator,
You know how easily
I am distracted,
how easily my mind wanders
or, worse, entertains less than holy thoughts.

I trust Your ever-present
and exceedingly abundant grace
will help me stay focused
on You and You alone.
Bless this time of prayer
dear Lord,
that it may be fruitful
for my soul.

And help me also
during the day
by granting me the grace
to insure that

my actions
and
my prayers
are
in harmony.
Let everything
I do today,
beginning with this time of prayer,
move me closer
to being one with You
in thought, word, and deed. Amen.

A Journey through Weakness

O God, help me follow
wherever You lead me.

I believe my spiritual life
is essentially a journey
in which I move from what I am
to what I will become.
I am just beginning
to learn that life is
a journey through weakness.
The saints truly learned to live
when they began to explore
their own weaknesses.
By Your unmerited grace,
every experience of weakness
is an opportunity for growth
and renewed life.
Weaknesses transformed by
the reality of Christ's love
become life-giving virtues.

The emptiness I often feel stems
from not realizing
I am made for communion
with You.
If I am not growing toward
unity with You,
my God,
I am then growing apart
from You.
Help me learn
to be still,
to be humble
in order to move into
a greater union with You.
Only in stillness and humility
can I enter into
a dialogue with You,
sweet Jesus.
I need to bring to You
what I am
so that in time
I might become
more like what You are.

In following you, Lord Jesus,
I have seen with my own eyes
in so many places around the world
how life is filled to overflowing
with pain and struggle.
Your way leads to the Cross,
and it doesn't offer
an easy way around it.
To become Your disciple
means accepting
a spirituality of the cross
and renouncing
a spirituality of glory.

You humbled yourself
in order to love me.
You gave of yourself
in order to love me.
Help me give myself
in order to love You
and all of creation.

In the Desert

At some point in time
God calls each of us
into the desert.
The desert is a place
of discipline,
which we need
but don't want,
and so we avoid it.
In the desert,
under the blazing sun,
all our weaknesses
are made clear.
We look around
and see the vastness
of nothing.
We do not know
which way to go.
In the desert,
our need for God
is also made clear.

In the desert,
we grow weary,
we lose hope.

We can't quench
our own thirst,
we know no pleasure.
All around is only
a void that stretches out
beyond our sight.
The day turns to night.

The arid, parched landscape
can only be watered by God.
God's water is sweet,
God's manna is tasty.
In the desert,
God's love is
our only comfort.
In the desert,
God's spirit
transcends the bleakness
in the depths of our souls
and we can see
beauty and tenderness.
In the desert,
ideas about God
give way to God.

O Lord, help me
not evade the desert,
not flee the pain of life,
the suffering that not even
Your beloved Son avoided.
Help me enter
the desert of silence,
the desert of surrender,
the desert of doubt,
the desert of sorrow and loneliness
so I can be nourished

by Your loving Word alone,
which is the only source of
true refreshment
and lasting peace.

Between Night and Day

As each new day dawns,
God's light gives us
a renewed pledge
of God's love,
a fresh beginning
that is pure gift,
a gift meant to be given away
during the day.

In the silence between night and day,
I feel God's grace and peace
and am commissioned
to become an instrument
of that very same grace and peace.
In the splendor of new light,
God's love and mercy are revealed.

O God help me to see
the radiance of Your light
and show me this day
how to be a servant of Your peace.
Help me, O God, to share
the delicate, intoxicating fragrance
of Your mercy and love
with those whose lives
are lived on the shadowy
and dismal margins,

with those whose days
see no happiness,
with those whose days
end without hope.

First and Foremost

O Lord, my mind and heart
are centered on so many things
other than You.
Mostly good things,
but not You.
Help me this day
to desire You
first and foremost,
and not to be distracted
by all the things
that pull me
this way and that way,
fragmenting my being.
Teach me this day, O Lord,
how to forget
my fears and anxieties,
and put all my trust and hope
in You alone.

I Hand it All to You

Oh my God, help me
to stop picking away
at the sore of my guilt
over my past misdeeds,
the many times

I failed to love.
Help me instead
fix my gaze on
Your endless love.

Help me see
how my sins are
merely manifestations
of my own inner emptiness
and an indication
of how far I am from You,
the true source of love.

I give you, my God,
everything that is within me.
I also surrender
all of my past.
I hand it all to You
and accept your
total forgiveness,
your overflowing mercy,
and your boundless love.

I also give You
all the wounds life
has inflicted on me.
Give me, please, the grace
to look at them honestly,
to feel them fully,
and then entrust them
to your divine care.
Help me also forgive
all who have harmed me,
and allow me to forget
the painful memories
that only allow the harm to live.

This day, I see my past,
my faults, my wounds, my shame,
and I let them go.
I give them to You.
I seek your Spirit
in order to have
the faith and strength
to live fully
in the present day,
consciously aware
of each precious,
life-giving moment.

In My Nothingness

Only through humble eyes
can God be seen.
I am nothing;
God is everything.
But in my nothingness,
God gives me everything.
Humility helps
shatter illusions.
Humility is the truest form
of honesty.
It sees our weaknesses
and vulnerabilities.
Humility allows God
to transform our weaknesses
into strengths.

Humility is a pathway
to prayer.
Prayer is the doorway

to the heart,
the center of our being,
the place where we can
let go, let go of
pretense, pride, ego
and a host of things
blocking us from
the true source of life,
the true source of love,
God.
In the innermost
chamber of the heart
we see the dissonance
between the Spirit of God
and our spirit;
it is here we struggle
to dissolve that disharmony.
In the safety
of the heart
we can let go of fear
and we can
risk change.
In the heart,
conflict gives way
to harmony.
In the heart,
what's mine
becomes God's.
In the heart,
humility becomes
holiness.

Present Moment

"I Am,"
says God.
God did not say,
"I Was,"
or
"I Will Be."
In saying
"I Am,"
God is saying,
"I am present."

Am I present?
Or do I live
in the past,
replaying old scenes,
clinging to old wounds?

Am I present?
or do I live
in the future,
chained to useless fantasies
and baseless fears?

God is beyond time
and always present.
But we look away.
We look back
and are hurt.
We look ahead
and are terrorized.

In this present moment,
God is facing us.
In this present moment,
we will no longer be
victims of the past
or be
paralyzed by the future.

In this present moment
we can face God.
In this present moment
we can encounter God.
Oh God, help me
be
in this present moment.
Oh God, help me
see
in this present moment
You.
Oh God, help me
see You
in all I do,
in all my encounters,
in all the people I meet,
in all of creation.

ꝯy Soul Is ꝯhirsting for God

My soul has been wounded,
gravely so.
I am unable to heal myself.
You, O God, alone know
the source of my hidden ailments.
You know all my doubts, my confusions,
and the endless contradictions that spring
from my meager life.
You know my weaknesses,
my faults and my many failures.
You, O God, alone know
how parched and dry
my inner life is,
how I desperately thirst
for the only water
that can quench my intense longing.

I am comforted by the fact
that I know that You know
that I do want to know You
more fully,
to love You
more completely.
I truly do want
to be one with You
and to please You always.
But through my fault,
my most grievous fault,
I do not always act
as I wish to act.
I am not always aware
of Your presence
because I am too focused

on myself,
on my own wounds,
my own ideas,
my own selfish desires.
I am bounced around
too easily
by the thoughts of others
that appear to sparkle with truth
yet often are merely distractions
or, worse, dreadful diversions.
The path to Your door
and the fullness of life
is straight and narrow,
yet I keep veering off onto
cul-de-sacs of empty promises
and phantom illusions.

My God, my God
your way is so confusing
and hard to follow.
Yet it is so clear
and so easy to follow.
You simply and only want
me to love,
always, everywhere, everyone.
You want me to do as You do,
to make myself invisible and silent,
to make myself weak and poor,
to give myself away, completely
and without reservation,
so that only You can shine.

In my time of early morning prayer,
in the stillness and silence
that blankets the coming of dawn,
I get it and want to do it.

But then I get up,
and I am no sooner out of the house,
and my resolve begins to dissolve.
I argue and become petty.
My temper flairs,
my joy flees.
Resentments rise,
faith falls.
Doubts and confusions
encamp around me.
By nightfall,
I have been reduced to ashes,
a smoldering heap of anguish
tormented by my own mediocrity.

But You love me,
always, everywhere,
even when my behavior
turns its back on You.

O my God, I beg You
to heal my wounds,
to help me go through this day
more in harmony with You.
Help my faith and actions
have smaller and smaller gaps
between them.
Give me, please, my God,
the grace to pause
often during the whirlwind
of the day,
and tell You that I love You,
that I need You,
that I want to do Your will.
Shower the parched, dry, waterless
terrain of my inner life

with Your abundant grace
that will keep You
in my heart and mind
all day long,
especially during those times
when I am at my weakest.

I know it is impossible for You
to withhold Your love from me.
It is the one thing You can't do,
for loving is the essence of Your being.
Yet all too often, sadly,
it is possible for me
to reject Your perfect
and all-embracing love.
I don't mean to reject Your love,
for who would reject
the most perfect love of all.
But I do sometimes forget it,
I get distracted
or beset by doubts
or desires for things
not rooted in You.
Please, dear Lord,
increase Your unmerited grace
during those moments
of weakness and confusion.

You know and I know
that I will fail again.
Oh, how that thought pains me.
Please continue to reach out
Your hand and help me
get back up.

Without You
I am
nothing.

With You
I lack
nothing.

You are the fullness of life,
the fullness of love.
In You is endless mercy,
endless compassion,
endless forgiveness.
You alone are holy,
You alone are Lord.

Lord, have mercy on me
a lowly sinner.

A Soothing Ray of Light

O God, help me let go of
everything in my life
and all that I expect and wish for.
I know that You have
the best plan for me,
and I am trying
to give You everything:
my life, my time, my possessions
and my aspirations.
Help me to wait upon You
and not take matters
into my own hands.
I want to give You my all
and I believe

with all my heart and strength
that You will take care of me,
far and above anything I could ever do.
I love you Lord,
and I want all of my life
to be my gift to You.
Help me, please, dear Lord,
let go of everything
that keeps me from being
more fully united to You.

Lord, help me grow
in humility,
help me to confess
my own brokenness.
Help me move out of my world
of illusion and self-created desires
and into Your universe
of love, joy and peace.

Lord, I cry out for healing.
Transform my brokenness,
I beg You,
into a new life in You,
the true source
of strength and wholeness.

Help me, Lord, remove everything
that blocks me from joyfully living
the good news of the paschal mystery.
O awesome and transcendent God,
free me from the slavery of my sinfulness.

In my prison of darkness,
Your unmerited grace
is a soothing ray of light.

The Narrow Path

O God, you know
I want to fulfill
your holy desire
for my life,
want to take the path
You wish I would take.
O God, you know also
that I not only stray
from the narrow path
you have chosen for me
but that sometimes
I choose to take
a totally different path.

And you, O Lord, are so
gentle and kind
You give me the freedom
to go the way I wish to go.
But more than that,
You still walk with me,
still love me
and long to guide me.
Your gift of grace
makes my new path
a new way to You.

You never abandon me
no matter which way I go.
And when I go the wrong way,
a way that would
lead me away from You,
You do not withdraw Your grace
and still gently offer me

opportunities to turn around,
to change my misguided way.
You are a God of endless chances.

Thank you, dear Lord,
for turning my life around.
Please help me
stay on the narrow path
back to Your heart.
Please help me
embrace
more and more of You.

Bitter Cross

O sweet Lord
I want so very much
to avoid the bitter cross
You ask me to carry,
the cross of putting aside
everything that is outside
the realm of Your love.
Actually, nothing is outside
the realm of Your love,
because You so long for us,
so thirst for us,
that You follow us
into the darkest corners
of our lives
looking to embrace us
with Your mercy and compassion.
Yet I so often
want to embrace things
that You find
unhealthy and unfitting
for a seeker of God.

O Lord help me see, feel and know
that outside of You
there is nothing of any worth,
and that with You
all is priceless.
Help me nail to the cross
the secret things in my heart
that I must sacrifice
in order to follow You
more closely
and love You
more dearly.

A More Suitable Chamber

O Lord, help me to renew
my innermost being.
I stumble and fall often.
My many failures
disappoint me.
But You never treat me
as I deserve.
You close your eyes
to my faults.
I trust in your endless
mercy and compassion.
But I need your help
to truly purify
my deepest being,
to create there
a more suitable chamber
for Your spirit to reside.

Endless Love

You alone, my God, are faithful
to your promises.
I know You are with me,
walking beside me,
and I have no reason
to fear or doubt . . .
but I am weak
and need Your strong arm.

I appeal to Your gentleness,
O God of mercy.
I seek Your divine help,

O God of compassion.
I cling to Your faithfulness,
O God of endless love.

My Plans

O God, You know my plans.
Help me hear Your plan for me.
Help me know when my plans
are rooted in my false self,
the "me" that does not see
it's own weakness and pride.
Help me never forget that
the only bread I need is You.

My Refuge

God, you have been my refuge
from year to year;
You are my refuge
from day to day,
even from hour to hour.
Blessed are you, Lord.
Show me, I beg, what You want
me to do,
who You want me to become.
I am Yours.
Yet, I still need to learn Your will,
learn what You desire for me,
for you are my God.
You are the source and sustainer
of all life.

Yet I still stray from You.
You are the only light
to lead me out of my own darkness.
Lord have mercy on me a sinner.

The Canvas of My Soul

Oh God, I have not yet
truly begun to paint
the canvas of my soul.
Help me find the vivid brush strokes of
love, tenderness, compassion,
wonder, poetry and purity
needed to create a portrait
inspired by You
to be given as a gift
to all who see it.

Help me replace
the dark, hidden tones
of my life
with the numinous hues
that reveal harmony and balance.
Have the borders
of my canvas
not be so small
as to exclude
the richness and diversity
of all humanity
and the endless paths
to the divine.

PART TWO

Poetic Reflections

"*Love is the most powerful and still the most unknown energy of the world.*"

—TEILHARD DE CHARDIN

Live Love

Contemplation and poverty
are natural partners.
Contemplation helps us to see,
to see both inside us
and to see around us.
Our contemplative vision improves
as our lives become
more simplified.
Our lives are cluttered
with so much stuff,
and we are so easily distracted
by so many things,
that our spiritual vision
is severely diminished.

We live in a thick fog
of materialism and escapism.
Poverty and simplicity
help us see
what is important,
help us see
another's need,
help us see
injustice and suffering,
helps us see
the need to be free
from all attachments
that limit our freedom
and ability to love.

Contemplation leads
to communion.
The world is divided
into two camps:

the rich and the poor.
And between those two camps
there is no communication,
no shared life, no communion.
The rich and the poor
are strangers,
and their mutual isolation
gives birth to
misunderstanding and mistrust.
And the gap between
the rich and the poor
grows wider and deeper
by the hour.

Jesus condemned
the unnatural and unjust division
between the rich and the poor,
because the division causes
pride, envy, jealousy,
self-centeredness and loneliness.
The Kingdom of God,
Jesus tells us,
is about unity,
reconciliation, harmony,
peace and love.
The Kingdom of God
is about oneness.

Jesus calls us
to a life of communion,
communion with God
and communion with each other.
And the life of communion
helps us grow
in knowledge and love
of God and each other.

Jesus is the bridge
between the rich and the poor,
the bridge between
earth and heaven.
The cross of Christ
reconciles us to God
and each other,
and is a lived example
of self-emptying love.

Contemplation and communion
lead to action,
call us to the margins of society,
to the American urban jungles
of deprivation, crime and violence,
to the dark corners around the world,
where people live in massive slums
of overwhelming need.
And in these deprived places,
we not only give life,
but life is also given to us.
It is here
we see for the first time
the oneness
that has always been there,
though obscured by
our blindness.

Through contemplation
we learn to see.
Through communion
we learn to share.
Through action
we learn to love.

Be still.
Know God.
Live love.

Messy Moments

God is not hiding
in the corner of an empty church.
God is hidden in the endless stream of
busy, messy, mundane moments of everyday life.
And God is also hidden
in the many tragedies
that dot the vast landscape of humanity.
God is not beyond the clouds;
God is on the ground,
down in the gutter with us.

What We Are

The more we worship God
the more we grow in humility.
The more we grow in humility
the more gentle we become.
The more gentle we are
the less aggressive we become.
Stripped of aggression
the more pure we are.
As we grow in purity
the more receptive we are
to the gift of God's spirit.
The more filled we are
with God's spirit

the more loving and compassionate
we become.

Nothing can separate us
from love
if love
is not what
we have
but what
we are.

In My Brokenness

At the heart of every life there is
a deep, mysterious pain.
No one can avoid it or cure it.
My faith tells me
that God loves me in my brokenness.
And that God loves me fully and unconditionally,
without a hint of reservation,
even in my darkest, most sinful, most unloving moments.
God does not demand perfection;
God gives love.
The essence of faith is trust . . .
trusting in God's undivided, unmerited love.

A Silent Symphony

Before bed at night
surrender the anxieties
of the day
into the tender hands

of God's love.
Rest in peace;
arise in hope.

To bring to a new day
yesterday's pain and failures
is the easiest way
to darken the new day.

Every sunrise
is accompanied by
a silent symphony
of hope and peace,
which can only be heard by
a surrendered heart.

Each Moment

We begin each day
without knowing
how it will end.
But in that very beginning
we see the promise,
see the road to fulfillment.

In Haiti, I often sit
on the balcony
in the pre-dawn darkness
sipping coffee
and watching the sunrise
slowly and faithfully bringing
the fresh promise
of new hope.

The radiant hope of God's light
is truly present
at the dawn of each new day,
yet we are often
too sleepy
or too distracted
to see it.
Each moment
of the coming day
is a rebirth,
each moment
a Christmas miracle.

And each moment
presents us with
an opportunity
to become more Christ-like,
to respond to every person,
especially every poor or suffering person,
and to every situation,
with love and compassion.

Each moment
gives us
an opportunity
to be instruments
of grace and peace.
Each moment
offers us
an opportunity
to reject our
culture of death
and promote
a culture of life.
Each moment
presents us

a chance
to transform our hearts
and our society.

Each moment
gives us an opportunity
to be embraced by
the tenderness of God's love,
an abundant love
that is generously extended
to all beings
without exception.

All of creation is
one Holy Family,
which we,
in our pride and selfishness,
have torn asunder.
As God's children,
we are, as Paul says,
"holy and beloved,"
and we are called to express
"heartfelt compassion, kindness,
humility, gentleness and patience"
in our relationship
with each other
and all of creation.

But we do not.
I do not.
But that is
the goal of our journey.
Each day
we need to
redirect our efforts,
check the maps

of our inner lives.
I do so by scribbling down
some of the avalanche of thoughts
that dot my days
and the meager periods of
stillness and silence
that I try to carve out of each day.
I record my scattered thoughts
primarily for myself.
I need them.
Desperately.
It is so easy for me
to forget the lessons
I have learned,
so easy to forget
the gentle whispering
I faintly and occasionally hear
in the stillness of
prayer and contemplation.

And, perhaps more shockingly,
it is often easy for me to forget
the pain and suffering
I've seen in the many horrific slums
I've filmed around the world
and that I see every day
here in misery-plagued Haiti.
I need to be constantly reminded
of the self-emptying love of Christ,
which I am called to imitate
in my own halting, clumsy, limited
way.

Genesis

We live in
a constant state
of genesis,
always changing,
always evolving,
always being born anew.
Today we begin again.
This very moment
is pregnant
with new possibilities
for growing
in God,
with God,
through God.
Today is
a new creation.

Designed to Be Shared

To think of God
outside the context of
love and community
is not to think about God.
For God is love,
and God's love,
as illustrated in the Trinity,
is communal,
designed to be shared
with all
and without exception.

In the Risen Humanity of Christ

In the risen humanity of Christ,
I find peace and love.
But it is not enough for me
to simply experience
that peace and love
within myself
or only for myself.
It is something that
must be shared with
all of humanity,
all of creation.

In every encounter,
in every relationship,
I should attempt to convey
the risen humanity of Christ
through my words and deeds.
And this experience
of the risen humanity of Christ
makes all things always new,
always presenting fresh opportunities
to transform ourselves
and our world
by following
the self-emptying example of Jesus
who constantly renews
everything he touches
because he is always
pointing us back to God,
back to the true source of life.

In a Fog

There is nothing
so steady and relentless,
so committed and enduring,
so firm and unwavering
as God's love
for us.
Over and over again,
in story after story,
Jesus tells us that
the defining characteristic of God
is not anger
but love.

Yet we stumble around
in a fog of
misplaced guilt
and wrong attachments.
As children of God,
we are called to be
people of love,
people who accept
God's love
and people who transmit
God's love.

Poverty of Spirit

Poverty of spirit
is a manger
of gentle receptivity
that allows the Divine
to be born within us.
To be wholly present
to God,
with all of our heart,
mind and soul,
we must be
poor in spirit.

Poverty of spirit
is far more than
material poverty.
While material poverty
may help to facilitate
poverty of spirit,
it is nonetheless important
to realize that a person
without possessions

can still be possessed
by a craving for things.
It is the craving
that makes us restless,
distracting our hearts and minds
from being present
to God alone.
Poverty of spirit
frees us from being
divided by false idols
and uncurbed passions.

Poverty of spirit
does not refer to
an economic condition.
It reflects the human reality
that we are poor
before God
and we need to
radically depend
on God alone
for true fulfillment.

We must be on guard
not to confuse
the necessities of life
with luxuries.
The humble simplicity
that embodies poverty of spirit
stands in stark contrast
with the unbridled pursuit of
comfort, power,
pleasure, and riches,
which permeates a society
that prizes possession
as a good in itself.

Poverty of spirit
is a means of maintaining
a continual attitude
of dying to self
without succumbing
to self-hatred
or causing a lack of self-esteem.
We need to die to self
because it is the only way
to be fully alive to God.

The Gift of Love

At the heart of love
is a desire (eros) to be
one with the beloved.
This passionate desire
for unity
is so strong it feels
the absence of the beloved.
Love wants what it is missing
so badly it hurts.
But while love desires
the love of its beloved,
love also wants
to give itself away
to its beloved.
This gift of love (agape)
exists side-by-side
with the desire for love (eros)
within our hearts.
It is the very union of
eros and agape
that love reaches its fulfillment.

It is not enough
to simply desire God.
We need to give ourselves
to God.

God loves us,
wants to be one with us.
But we shunned that love,
turned our backs on God.
God's passionate desire for us,
even after feeling the pain
of our rejection,
is joined with God's gratuitous gift
of endless love to us
in the person of Jesus.

In Christ,
humanity and divinity
are wedded in
everlasting love.

A Crowded Subway

Make each new day
holy.

Individual holiness
allows God
to appear in our midst,
on our streets, in our homes,
on a crowded subway or bus,
in a factory and an office,
at the beach or a ballpark—
anywhere where humans are.
Holiness makes God visible.

The Gospel asks us to live
without embellishment or pretense,
to live without anxiety
and to live free from
all illusions of success.

Ambition should be confined
to topping yourself.

Seek wonder,
not success.

Open Hands

Approach God with
open hands,
a searching mind,
and a loving heart.

Our relationship with God
requires growth
in humility, simplicity, and poverty.

Prayer is essentially
loving God,
which is why
we need to deepen
our prayer life
in order to
deepen our love.

A simple heart is
a heart where God is.
A simple heart is

a pure heart,
a heart willing
to surrender itself
to the will of God.

Barriers and Boundaries

"Surrender" is a positive word
in the language of spirituality.
It allows us to receive
the gift of new life
in God's saving action.

God wants to
impregnate us
with love.
All we need to do
is surrender and say,
with Mary,
"Thy will be done."

Poverty is
letting go.

Not to let go,
and surrender
to the will of God,
is to know
misery and despair.

It is not important
what we do;
what is important is
what we drop.

We need to drop
the barriers and boundaries
that separate us
from ourselves and from others.

Mary feeds
the immortality
of my soul.

In one basic way,
we should all strive
to imitate Mary, because Mary
did what we all must do:
bear Christ in the world.

Authentic Transformation

Outside the inevitable suffering
caused by death and accidents,
most suffering bubbles up out of
our craving for transitory things
and our worldly attachments.

It is easy to become attached
to the kind of secure certainty
peddled by religious fundamentalism.
But this kind of "knowing"
is a roadblock
to true knowing.
Clinging to the
comfort of certainty
is just as bad as
all our temporal attachments.

It is difficult for God's Word to enter
our inner temple
because its entrance is blocked
by our endless array of attachments.
In order to be heard,
God requires
from us
silence and detachment.

Without daily contemplative silence
it is impossible to have
a true encounter
with God's Word within us,
where authentic transformation
begins.

A Moment of Grace

Humility is the heart of Christianity,
and the gateway to prayer.
Prayer is being present.
Without prayer,
God dies in our hearts.
Transformation is a daily event.
Every moment is
a moment of grace—
if my eyes and heart are open.
Contemplation requires
tranquility and patience.
To be a contemplative is
to be receptive to
the divine Word.

Kids at Play

Seriousness stifles spirituality.
Jesus said we must be like children:
carefree, energetic and playful.
Children are alive and radiant;
they live in the moment.

Spiritual growth requires a measure of
relaxation, listening, and humor.

We tend to visualize Christ
with a sober countenance.
We need to remember that Christ
also smiled
because his soul was imbued
with joy.

The holy is not confined
to the solemn.
Everything is holy.
God lives
in laughter and in suffering.

Naked Before God

No one can see the depths
of their own poverty.
Without words or thoughts,
I must force myself
to stand naked before God.
Only then can I learn
to say truthfully:
"Blessed are those who know
that they are poor."
Coming face to face
with my own total poverty
is the only way
to come face to face with God
and find true enlightenment.

If you ask God a question,
God will respond.
And God responds
at the level you are willing to receive.

The problem isn't God.
The problem is me.

If you take God seriously,
you eventually will have
a wrestling match
with God.

Daunting Yet Essential Questions

Who am I?
I mean deep down inside,
at the very core of my being . . .
who am I?
Is my true identity,
my true self,
something created
in the mind of God,
or is my identity
something shaped
by the external forces
of my birth, my family, my friends
and the very circumstances of my life,
such as where I live and work,
and maybe even by what I eat?
Is my identity formed
by chance or choice . . .
or the hand of God?
Did God have a purpose for me?
And if so,
is my identity inexorably linked
to that divine purpose?

These are daunting
yet essential questions.
Answers seem
speculative and suspect
at best.
My experience tells me
God is real.
Furthermore,
my experience reveals
that God is love.

If God is love,
and I therefore came from love,
it seems logical that
my true identity
will only be revealed
in the perfection of Love
within me.

Linguistic Limitation

We toss about
the word "God"
so freely and
with such flourish
that we deny the reality
that the word names something
that is beyond all naming,
beyond all comprehension.
We seem to easily dismiss
(or not even understand)
that the very word "God"
is a linguistic limitation
that imposes on
the reality of the entity
it is feebly attempting to name.

God emerges out of
primordial silence
and is forever silent.
We know nothing
of the experience of God;
we can only experience
something of God
living in us.

God is in all things,
but God's relationship
to all things
is expressed in silence.
Our experience of God
is beyond words;
we experience God
in silence.
Silence is
the breath of God.

Silence is a vital part
of the natural cycle of creation;
it is a time of gestation,
lying fallow and renewal.

The Notes of Grace

Life has become so
frenetic and fragmented
that
stillness and wholeness
have become
the impossible dream.

In stillness and silence
you can hear
the notes of grace
singing in the breeze.

The Silent Voice of God

Our real pilgrimage
is into the depths of silence...
and leads to a true light.
The quest for God
is a journey,
a pilgrimage to
the depths of the soul.
The quest requires
a listening heart,
an ear quickened
to the silent voice of God,
and a vigilant spirit
actively waiting and watching.
To be a pilgrim is
to live on life's threshold,
walking on the edge of reality,
striving for what lies beyond
the reality
we see with
our flawed human eyes.

A Wordless Noise

Listening to God
requires silence.
Silence is more than
not speaking.
There is within us
a wordless noise
which also needs
to be muted.
A silent listener

tunes out
all exterior and interior
chatter
in order to be
totally attentive to
the soundless voice of God,
actively listening
and responding to
the very Source
of his or her Being.
It is only in deep silence
that we can perceive
the reality of God
and the world around us.

Hidden in the Ordinary

Listen to the silence of nature
and you will hear a symphony
singing the praises of God.

In the incubator of silence,
wisdom and tolerance are born.

Leave room for the unexpected,
the moment of insight.
Don't shut the door
on tiny epiphanies.

Everyday carries the experience
of presence and absence.

Prayer helps you see
the extraordinary
hidden in the ordinary.

Our prayer life
needs to move from being
mechanical and extrinsic
to being mystical and intrinsic.

The only thing standing between
me and God
is me.

My sins expose my fallibility...and
my complete dependence
upon God alone.

Meek and Humble

Humility is
the cornerstone of repentance.
Sadly, humility's stock
has declined in our time.
Instead, we value a sense of pride,
a sense of self-glorification,
a sense of self-righteousness.
Today, many people view humility
as a sign of weakness.
How easily we forget
the words of Christ:
"Learn from me for I am
meek and humble in heart."

Repentance,
deeply rooted in humility,
is a return to
the right order of things.
Repentance is
the path out of exile.

Repentance is more than
"pleading guilty"
to transgressions.
Repentance needs to acknowledge
our alienation
from God,
our failure
to enter fully into the joy
of communion with the Divine.

Repentance is not merely a response
to a spiritual indictment;
it must also be a response to the fact
that we have strayed
from the glory of God.

The Grace of Forgiveness

Our main job in life
is reconciliation . . .
with God,
with ourselves,
with each other,
and with all of creation.
To be a follower of Christ
is to be open
to the grace of forgiveness.

Christ asks us to forgive
those who have offended us;
he goes so far as to say
we must love our enemies.
Reconciliation is the key
to personal liberation.

Hurt and Angry

A friend hurt me.
I am finding it difficult
to pray for him.
But I must persevere,
for in praying for him
I will free myself
from the bondage of anger
which will only destroy me.

Hatred is
death to the soul.

Our culture's preference
for self-affirmation
has transformed forgiveness
into a sign of weakness.

True Fellowship

Mercy is an essential ingredient
of Christian spirituality.
It is a sign
of God's perfection and care.

Mercy is the generous sharing
with others
God's gift of mercy,
which we have experienced.

Mercy allows forgiveness
of failures, hurts and sins.
Mercy creates

the possibility
of true fellowship
among all people;
without mercy,
genuine community
is not possible.

Mercy turns discrimination
into reconciliation.
Mercy gives us eyes
to see all people
as images of God
and prompts us
to share our lives and resources
with each other.

Mercy rejects no one
and welcomes everyone
to the Eucharistic table.

To Love Truly

We can only love truly
when our hearts are
free of the self-centered desires
of pride, ambition, and lust.

For me,
the choice
between
thinking about
God
and surfing the internet
for images

that will feed
my lustful
desires,
God usually
loses.

How can God lose?
Only when
I prevent
God from
winning.

God's Goodness

My life's journey,
now into its eighth decade
and slowing down,
has shown me
just how capable I am
in making inappropriate choices
and engaging in harmful behavior.

But God is more powerful
than my shortcomings,
and no negative behavior of mine
slows down God's
boundless goodness.
God's goodness
helps me triumph over
my far too numerous failures.

The Bloated Belly of Poverty

Despite my external
appearance of affluence,
I am a poor man,
a blind beggar.

After spending more than four years writing a book on St. Francis, I knew in the recesses of my heart that I did not really understand the saint's love of poverty. In the Fall of 1999, after delivering the manuscript for The Sun and Moon Over Assisi *to the publisher, I set out on a quest that would take me deeply into the bloated belly of poverty. With the support of the Minister General of the Order of Friars Minor, I spent more than two years documenting the plight of the poor in some of the most horrific slums on earth for a photo/essay book on the Christian response to global poverty titled* When Did I See You Hungry?

At the dawn of the Spring of 2002, I delivered that book to the publisher... and I was still in the dark about poverty, its causes and remedies.

But I've come
to a much clearer understanding
of my own poverty.
My own weakness.
My own sinfulness.
My own need for
forgiveness and mercy.
The poor have taught me
to see that the real stuff of life
is found in relationships.

A Franciscan friar
who lives among the poor

in the slums of Philadelphia
once said to me,
"In the end,
the only thing that matters
is the Lord...
and each other." Amen.

I am truly poor.
I need God.
And I need you.
We need each other...
and we need God.
I am learning
how vitally important
it is to spend time
deepening my relationship
with God,
first and foremost.
And as that relationship
grows stronger,
I have the strength
to embrace you
and your weaknesses
and failures
more fully,
sharing with you the
love, forgiveness and mercy
I've received from God.

We are all poor,
blind beggars
who need to stretch out
open hands
to God
every day.

Pay Attention

The health of our interior life
rests upon our attentiveness.
We need to be able to
truly pay attention
in order to hear
the wordless voice of God
that is continually
drawing us into Oneness.

To be attentive,
we need to be
awake and alert
to the boundless grace
of the present moment.
Our lives have become
so splintered,
divided among
so many responsibilities,
so many demands
upon our time,
that most of us feel
frazzled and fatigued.

So much of modern technology,
designed to make things easier for us,
has in fact increased
the things that tug
for our attention.
The internet, cell phones,
lap-top computers, tablets,
Blackberries, iPads
and the ever-expanding
world of cable television

all squeeze every ounce of
stillness and silence out of life.
Life has become a blur,
a whirling dervish
of enticements and anxieties.
Entering into our interior life,
where we can encounter
the love and mercy of God,
is becoming
increasingly difficult.

A World of Hearts

The human heart
is drawn to God.
The language of the heart
is love.
Not soft, wimpy,
fleeting Hollywood-style love,
but a bold, deep,
penetrating love
that requires
openness and transformation,
a love that
perpetually gives
itself away.

We live in a world of hearts.
Sadly, most hearts are broken,
unloved and unable to love.
God wants to give us
new hearts,
mystical hearts
throbbing to love

and to be loved.
If you can imagine
a world of divinely
transformed hearts,
you will see
a world a peace,
a world of plenty
where no one goes hungry.
Such a world begins
within each of us,
if we are able
to shake off
the countless distractions
of modern life
and pay attention
to the silent voice of God.

Ḣeaven on Earth

Heaven is
a hard word
to pin down.
What it is
or where it is
is a mystery.
Perhaps the simplest way
to define it is:
heaven is
the reality of God.

Heaven touches earth
whenever we catch
a glimpse of God,
whenever we encounter God

in a truly real way.
Heaven can be found
in a tender touch,
in a glass of water,
a morsel of food
given to a hungry person.

Heaven is seen
in an act of kindness,
an act of compassion.
Heaven is the reality of Love,
self-emptying, self-sacrificing love.

We should not strive
to get to heaven;
we should strive
to be heaven.

The 20th century Carmelite nun
Blessed Elizabeth of the Trinity
said it best:
"I have found my Heaven on earth,
because Heaven is God
and God is in my heart."

Heaven is within all of us,
and all of us can be in heaven
if we enter our hearts,
encounter and experience God
and then become
God's ambassadors
of love and peace.

A Whirlwind of Noise

So much of life
distracts us from Life.
We live in a
whirlwind of noise.
Our homes and cars have
elaborate entertainment centers.
Cell phones allow us to talk
while driving or walking in the woods.
Cable and satellite TV serve up
news, sports and movies 24 hours a day.
Computers link us
to the feral internet and chat rooms
and web sites featuring triple X porn stars.
Ears without iPods are rare.
And of course, crass commercialism
is always screaming something at us,
insisting we need
what we don't need.

Finding silence is harder
than finding peace in the Middle East.
Our culture is so riddled
with turmoil and confusion
it's easy to seek refuge
in the noise of
mindless entertainment,
channel surfing through
endless hours of tedious programs.
We need to welcome the chance
to be alone with God;
but the barren silence scares us,
and we quickly miss
the security blanket of noise.

We need time alone
in order to be present to God.
We need a desert experience.
In the barrenness of the desert,
whether literal or figurative,
we can experience the fullness of life.
The desert is a place of silence
where we find the quiet to hear.

Stealing

Many people have
more possessions
than they need, -
while others
do not possess
enough to live.

Our possessions should be
used to sustain life.
And we have
a right to possess
whatever we need
to sustain life.
But we do not have
a right to acquire
more and more possessions
just to satisfy a need to possess,
to accumulate more and more things.

As channels of grace,
we must give away
what we receive.

Consuming more
than you need
is stealing
from those in need.

In God's eyes,
love and justice
are not separated.

Solidarity with the poor flows out of
solitude with the Almighty.

God's Gift

God's love is universal.
It is for all.
We need to recognize
the inalienable dignity
of every human being,
regardless of race, religion or nationality.
The inclusively of the Gospel
requires us
to love everyone,
especially those
living on the margins of society,
the poor, the outcasts,
the neglected and abandoned.

We need to make ourselves
poor with the poor,
to identify with their misery,
their grief, their sickness,
and even their death.
Only then will the poor feel loved

and, as a result, strengthened.
Only when we enter into
this kind of relationship
with the poor
is it possible for them
and others
to detect the divine-human solidarity
of the God-Man, Christ,
with all men and women.
Our lives need to reflect the reality
that God gave us
as gift to each other.

Turbocharged

Most Americans live
turbocharged lives
addictively driven
to pursue
status and possessions.
Our compulsive drive
for more
is making us sick.
Our frenzied lives
distract us from
what is truly important:
relationships with other people.

In the world of business,
greed has reached
epidemic proportions,
which is choking to death
the chances of true happiness.
We seek and want

more than we need.
We are so busy
getting more
we can't enjoy
what we have.

It is no wonder
depression is on the rise.
We must slow down
and curb our appetite,
and find creative ways
to create meaningful work
and a more equitable distribution
of wealth.

Addicted

We are victims of over-stimulation,
and have become addicted
to anything loud and fast.

Wholeness is attained
when we achieve freedom
from the greedy tendencies
of the ego
and its insatiable hunger
for possession.
A person becomes whole
when the self
learns how to be empty,
willing to lose itself
in order to enter into
a deep and rich
communion with others.

Through charity,
God lives in us
and we live in God.

Charity is
love animated.

The Still Point

The super-excited, over-stimulated
pace of life today
is way out of sync
with the way God operates.
God works without rush or noise
in stillness and silence.

While our lives are lived
in fast-forward,
Christ invites us to
"come apart and rest awhile."
We need to stop running
and find the still point
where God waits
to embrace us.

Silent and Attentive

Jesus often sought
the emptiness of the desert
to experience
a fuller union with God.
God never shouts

to be heard
over our noise.
Only silence gives God
a chance to speak.
To effectively listen to God
—or even to another human being—
one needs to be
silent and attentive.

If we are truly listening
to God or another,
truly paying attention,
there will be no hint
of self-reflective consciousness—
there will only be
silent receptivity.
To listen
is to be silent.

The primary purpose of prayer
is to lead
heart and mind
to stillness.
We need to
empty our hearts,
to sit in stillness.
Silence allows us
to live within,
helps us to concentrate
on the serious,
profound inner mysteries
of life.
Noise takes us out
of ourselves,
and distracts and scatters
our thoughts.

I need to spend
less time
trying to understand God
(which is an impossibility)
and more time
adoring God.

The Unity of Life

Silence is not simply
a wordless state;
it is an attentive
waiting.
Deep, spiritually-active silence
allows us to hear
the unity of life.
Silence stills
the intellect
and opens
the portal of the heart.
Holy silence
takes our humble prayers
to new and exalted heights
of contemplation.
Be still,
and hear
the voice of God.
It is in stillness
that we find
our emptiness,
the emptiness that can only be filled
by welcoming God
into our hearts.

Seeing my own
emptiness and impermanence
prompted me
to fall to my knees
and pray:

Oh sweet Lord,
I pray for the grace
to empty myself
of all that
is only me
so that I may
be filled with
what is
only You.

Disconnected

Television and the internet
have turned our interior dwellings
into shanty towns.
Instead of looking in,
they prompt us to look outward,
and we become
what we gaze upon.
When praying,
we turn away from ourselves
and turn toward God.

Long ago, in a remote village
in the south of France,
St. John Marie Vianney,
known as the Curé of Ars,
noticed an old farmer

who used to sit for hours
in the humble, empty church.
When the saint asked him
what he was doing,
the farmer replied:
"He looks at me and I look at him."

It really is that simple,
but modern life is
so connected to
so much
we are easily
disconnected from
the All.

Symphony of Life

Love is
the symphony of life.
It needs to be
practiced and played
every day.

God is
the composer,
Christ is
the conductor,
and we are
the performers.

The Heart of All Reality

The primary motivation
for God's incarnation
is God's goodness,
not human sinfulness.

The Incarnation is
an expression
of God's overflowing
love and mercy.
The Incarnation is also an expression
of God's poverty and humility.

Through the Incarnation we find
redemption and completion,
making it the heart of all reality.

A Different Point of View

The infancy story of Christ
tells us we can have
hope and joy,
can overcome
our immense loneliness
and can find
unity, integration, solidarity
and reconciliation of all,
with all.

At its root, there is only one reason
for the existence of poverty:
selfishness,
which is a manifestation of
a lack of authentic love.

Sadly, we tend to think of the homeless
as social nuisances.
Jesus had a different point of view
and suggested that the poor
are pathways to God.

By serving the poor
we are not only practicing
Christian charity,
we are also
reforming ourselves.

We don't have to solve
all the problems for the poor;
just being with them
goes a long way toward
lightening their burden.

The witness of love
lived in voluntary poverty
has the peaceful power
to change hearts.

Running from Poverty

Jesus chose to be poor.
We wish he hadn't.
We are embarrassed
by his poverty.
His poverty makes us
uncomfortable.
Jesus suggests that poverty
is a privileged path,
that the poor possess
an eminent dignity.
We don't get it.
We do not choose to be poor.
We run from poverty,
we hide from poverty.
Poverty makes us uneasy.

For us, there is nothing "blessed"
about being poor.
But the truth is:
I am poor.
I am in constant need.
I am impoverished by
my many weaknesses,
my many bad habits.

I'm at the age
when each day
I'm impoverished by
the lack of time
I have left
to do the things
I want to do.
To understand poverty,
one must enter
the poverty of another,
as Jesus entered
our poverty.

Our poverty is blessed
when we do not possess anyone
and we are free
to be possessed by everyone.
In my poverty,
I can possess Jesus . . .
and give Jesus away.

Guess Who's Coming to Dinner

The Gospels make it
abundantly clear
that God is
on the side of the poor,
the broken in body and spirit,
and the outcasts of society,
the lepers, the prostitutes, the orphans...
and today, we must add the addicted.

Jesus invited the poor and the outcasts
to sit at his banquet table.
Who are our dinner guests?

Am I a part of a system
of oppression of the poor?
Unless I stand with the poor,
the answer is "yes."

A Fertile Garden

Voluntary poverty
is rich
in spiritual grace
because it creates
an emptiness
where desire to be one with those
unjustly imprisoned
in chronic poverty
is intensified.
St. Clare of Assisi
considered poverty
as her most prized possession.

A desire for poverty
is synonymous with
a desire for
total surrender of the self,
a desire for God alone.
Poverty is a fertile garden
where the imitation of Christ
can flower.

A Field of Poppies

Our spirits need time to rest,
to wander in a field of poppies,
to soar with the sunrise,
to swing in a hammock.
Our spirits need time to simply do nothing,
which, oddly enough, will give us the ability
to do everything better.

Solitude gives us insight
into our deepest needs and feelings.

Tranquility of heart and mind
springs naturally from
the well of solitude.

God speaks in silence.

A State of Alert Stillness

Prayerful silence
is more than
a lack of words;
it is a state of alert stillness.
The point is not to rest,
but to concentrate and focus
the heart and mind on God.
Beneath the appearance of
passivity
is an active state of
alertness.

Silence is an expression
of love and strength.
Within the silence of our hearts
lies a mystery beyond our hearts.
In deep silence,
we are fully awake,
fully open and one with God.
To enter the silence of meditation
is to enter our own poverty
as we renounce
our concepts and intellect
and sit alert,
waiting to hear from God
even if we must wait a lifetime.

Prayer helps us transcend
our preoccupation with
the self,
and teaches us how to embrace
the other.

Grace prompts us to pray,
and praying opens us up
to even more grace.
Our journey to God begins
in earnest when we still
our senses, desires, and mind.
In stillness,
real movement begins.
Stillness stills unruly passions.
Contemplation quiets our restless,
relentless quest for sensual pleasure.

The cornerstone of the spiritual life
consists of: stillness, prayer,
love and self-control.

Friends with Myself

Solitude is not the same as withdrawal,
which has negative connotations.
Solitude has positive qualities.
In solitude, I stopped running from myself
and became friends with myself.
Solitude taught me
to enjoy my own company.

In solitude, I learned that I'm not alone;
moreover, it taught me
there is no such thing as aloneness.
Spiritual growth does not come
from fleeing the world,
but from entering into it fully.
However, for the sake of our spiritual health,
we each need periods of solitude.
And we also need to develop
an inner solitude
that can be entered
no matter where we are.

The Wonder of Creation

Our minds are never entirely open.
Sin closes our minds.

Our senses have become dulled
to the wonder of creation,
which we take for granted.

Technical skill and tangible results,
high priests of our age,
are of little worth in the spiritual life.

The spiritual life places a premium
on integrity and integration.

The mystery of life
cannot be solved
with scientific or psychological answers.
The key to the solution,
if there even is one,
is mystical.

The eternal confounds
everything
we say and do.

Life is littered
with conflicts
which cannot be resolved.

A Faint Echo

We were created
in, by and through
Love.
We were made
for intimacy
with God.

Intimacy with God
is at the heart
of all our searching
for human friendship and intimacy.
We become more fully human
only in relationship
to our ever-deepening

consciousness of
and abandonment to
God,
the true source of
fulfillment and love.

Happiness and peace
are found
in a self-emptying love
that is made tangible
in a relationship
with another.

Happiness and peace
are not found
in isolation.
We are communal beings,
the fruit of
communal love
made tangible
within the loving exchange
found in the triune God.

Human love is merely
a faint echo
of divine love.
Human love is
weak, imperfect and
prone to failure
because of our
engrained selfishness.

But every loving human relationship,
no matter how flawed,
teaches us
— if we are open and willing to learn –

about the constantly beckoning,
always giving,
ever deepening,
perpetually self-emptying
love of God.

Love is not merely
romance.
Love is a school
where you learn
to let go
of all that is not God
so you can be filled
with God.

When two become
one flesh
they begin to sense
the beautiful unity
of God
and begin to take
feeble steps toward
true self-emptying intimacy
for which each of us
was created.

We have turned
the words
"I love you"
into a trite expression
— spoken today, forgotten tomorrow –
but they are the most
powerful words
we can ever utter.
We long to hear those words,
words that God whispers every day.

A Journey Toward Understanding

As both a Byzantine Catholic
and a Franciscan Christian,
my understanding of the world
has a distinctly Christocentric character.
For me, personal communion with Christ
is at the center and heart of all reality.
I believe Christ is the Wisdom of God,
the "unknown and unseen" Sophia,
in whom the cosmos
was created and sustained.

That belief should not, however,
hinder me (but it often does)
from affirming the other as other,
from saying yes to the other,
from saying yes to everyone.

But this is not easy;
and this is why
authentic dialogue is difficult.
It is not easy to hold onto
the core of your beliefs
without denigrating
conflicting beliefs
held by people
of different faiths.
But we must.

The world's faiths speak
in uniquely different tongues
of a transcendent reality
common to them all.
Perhaps people of differing faiths
can each grow closer to God
by drawing closer to each other.
The path of peace is dialogue.
Dialogue transforms
a stranger into a friend.
Friends can unite
in the struggle against
poverty and evil.

Interfaith dialogue requires
that people of differing faiths
avoid dogmatic assertions
when speaking with each other.
Theological arrogance and rigidity
stifle any authentic exchange.
Nor will dialogue succeed
if our aim is selling
our theological perspective.
True dialogue requires
an honest mutual exploration
of our respective theologies
and felt experiences of God;
it's a journey toward understanding,
not convincing.

Walking and Working Together

Without peace among religions
there will never be peace among nations.
Moreover, without honest, open dialogue,
there will never be peace among religions.
The survival of humanity
is contingent upon people
of different faiths
learning to walk and work together.
They must work together
to build a just, merciful, and peaceful society.
Otherwise, the haters and extremists
will bring us to the brink of extinction.

Your Neighbor's Yard

The faults of my neighbor
must be of no concern to me
nor be the subject of my idle chatter,
whose only purpose is to spotlight
my virtuousness and flatter my ego.

Let words fly from your mouth
on the gentle yet strong
wings of humility.

Goodness, from a Christian perspective,
does not come from morality
but from communion
with God and neighbor.

The path to God
runs through
your neighbor's yard.

Given Away

The best way
to lovingly serve
our neighbor
is to take our eyes off ourselves,
to forget ourselves,
to become unimportant to ourselves,
and fix our eyes
and hearts and minds on Christ.
We must let go of
self-centeredness
to love with

true purity
under all circumstances.

Justice should be moved
by love
to meet the needs
of the poor.

The emerging global economy
has a strong tendency to foster
soulless consumerism and
mindless worship of technology,
and it often tramples the rights
of workers and the poor.
We need to be alert
to the human consequences
and social impact of globalization.

We must become
the poor Christ
offered up and given away.

Both the New and the Old Testament
reveal God's preferential love
for those the world ignores and rejects.

The despised and the unimportant
of the world
are loved unconditionally
by their Creator.

By loving the poor and insignificant
first and foremost,
God demonstrates
the extent and fullness
of Divine love
for all of creation.

The Beauty of All Life

We are slow to compassion
because we are quick to exploit
others for our own gain.

As we grow in compassion
we are able to see more clearly
the beauty of all life
and we also increase our desire
to transform everything ugly
into something beautiful.

Not So Amazing Grace

God's grace isn't often easy to see.
Heck . . . it not even easy to define.
Speaking about pornography,
someone once said they couldn't define it
but they would know if they saw it.
It seems we don't really see grace
except in retrospect . . . long after the fact.

Grace is really not so amazing;
grace is commonplace;
grace is happening all the time,
all around us,
because God is always present.

Our Father

The heresy of American Christianity
is rugged individualism.
We speak of "my rights" and
"my relationship with God."
We are self-centered and narcissistic.
The great prayer of Christianity begins:
"*Our* Father..."
We are connected,
our prayer is communal.

Know yourself
and forget yourself.

A Never-Ending Mystery

Christ is not complete
without diversity.
Each person expresses Christ
in a unique way.

God is a never-ending mystery.

Every person is
a word of
the Word.

God is not remote.
God is here,
with and for us.

God is relational.

God is self-giving.

God is humble
not regal.

Love requires freedom.
We need to be free
to choose love.

Creating Beauty

In the act of creation
we begin to approach
ever so dimly
the divine imagination.
It is important for each of us
to create something,
our own creative expression,
that is a mere fragment
of the creative explosion
birthed in the boundless
imagination of God.
Our very lives
can create beauty
by our very presence.

True Freedom

Humanity tends to view greatness
in relation to one's ability to dominate.
Jesus offers a different perspective.
For Him, greatness lies in the ability
to give oneself away.

The wonder of the universe
and the totality of our humanity
is within ourselves.
It is a gift of life
which we must give away
in order to possess it.

To be in communion
with God and each other
we must liberate ourselves
from ourselves,
from our hungry egos
in order to be free enough
to give ourselves
to the Other
and each other.

Time

Christ is not asking us
to be successful
or productive.
Christ is looking for us
to be present . . .
present to God (in prayer),
and present to each other,
present to each other

in acts of love and mercy,
especially present
to the poor and the suffering.

But we don't really take Jesus seriously.
We don't love our enemies.
We don't turn the other cheek.
We don't forgive 70 x 7 times.
We don't bless those
who curse us.
We don't share what we have
with the poor.
We don't put
all our hope and trust
in God.

We say: I am not a saint.
We say: This Gospel stuff
can't be meant for everybody.
We say: The Gospel is an ideal.

But the gospel is not merely an ideal.
The Gospel is the Way.

Today gives us
the chance to see
we have strayed
from the Way.

Today is a time for
self-examination,
a time for
repentance
a time for
acts of self-control
and acts of charity
through self-emptying.

Now is the time
to enter into
the suffering and death of Jesus
which opened the
reign of God's grace
and eternal life
to all humans.

Now is the perfect time
to take Jesus seriously.

No Time

We have plenty of time
to do the things
we want to do.

We don't have time to pray
because we don't
want to pray.

God and Cookies

I have a weakness for cookies.
God has a weakness for human beings.

We want a God who is knowable
but not too knowable.
If God is so knowable
as to be intimate with us -
which God is, thanks to the Incarnation -
God will ask things of us,
and this we do not want.

Confused about God?
Tell God you don't understand.

How easy it is to forget
to seek the help and guidance
of the Holy Spirit.

Everyone has access to God.

God gives you the grace you need
whenever you are ready to receive it.

A Luminous Creation

Asceticism plays a part
in the spiritual life
just as discomfort plays a part
in the natural life.
We do what we need to do
in order to fight cold and heat;
so also, we need to fight sin and weakness.
But compulsive asceticism is of no use.

At the very least, asceticism can be
an effective self-management tool.

When asceticism and mysticism wed,
the saints tell us they give birth
to a luminous creation . . . as long as both
are hidden with Christ in God.

A Big Vowel

God is a big vowel—we are little vowels.

Only God can satisfy the heart.

God wants to take upon Himself
all our cares—let Him.

Cast your care upon the Lord.
Put aside all useless care.

A Follower of Jesus

To be a follower of Jesus
is to prefer life over death.
To be a follower of Jesus
is to prefer peace over war.
To be a follower of Jesus
is to prefer freedom over oppression.
To be a follower of Jesus
is to prefer forgiveness over revenge.

To be a follower of Jesus
is to prefer reconciliation over alienation.
To be a follower of Jesus
is to prefer contrition over excuses.
To be a follower of Jesus
is to prefer helping over hurting.

To be a follower of Jesus
is to prefer humility over pride.
To be a follower of Jesus
is to prefer vulnerability over power.

To be a follower of Jesus
is to prefer weakness over strength.

To be a follower of Jesus
is to prefer letting go over acquiring.
To be a follower of Jesus
is to prefer mysticism over materialism.
To be a follower of Jesus
is to prefer silence over noise.
To be a follower of Jesus
is to prefer prayer over idle chatter.

The Throne of My Heart

Before any progress is made
along the spiritual path,
it seems essential that we consider
exactly where our affections lie.

Am I willing to give up all
or even much
of what I cherish?
Or more basically,
can I relegate all
the things and people
whom I consider important in my life
to second place,
so that God alone occupies
the throne of my heart.

The ego's need to control reality
is as determined and uncontrollable
as a wild bronco.
It must be tamed.

An egocentric search
for self-fulfillment
is doomed to failure.

The cycle of addictive
desire and disappointment
robs us of happiness.

A Tiny Space

Within the tiny space
of our cluttered hearts
lies the infinite presence and love
of the all-merciful God

To pray is simply
to remain open
to the inflowing
of divine love.

To pray is to be in
a relationship
with God.

The more time
we spend in prayer
the deeper that relationship
will become.

Where Love Is

When we are enslaved
by obsessive desires
we are not free to pray.

When our interest in
power, money and material things
is greater than
our longing for God,
we are still far from
authentic prayer.

The deeper we journey
into prayer
the less interested we are
in thoughts rooted in
worldly desires and sensory perceptions.

Our prayer should be dressed
in reverence and humility,
unsoiled by a mind
still cluttered, impassioned and impure.

Calm the restlessness of your mind
by mindfulness of your breathing
and by acts of compassion and mercy.

The altar of our spirit
should be unadorned
and free of
false and unhealthy desires.

We must imitate God
who stoops down in mercy
to touch us.

So we too must
stoop down in mercy
to touch others . . .
even those who live far away.

The spiritual life
is a twofold journey . . .
an inward movement
to the depths of our being
and the source of Love
and an outward movement
to the broken world,
the margins of society,
where love is manifested
in acts of kindness.

Money Talks

God wants us to listen
to our hearts.
We want to watch
our bank accounts.

There is more than money
in our wallets.
Our wallets have a voice.
Our wallets speak
whenever we buy something.

Made by Love

We do not know peace,
because we do not know love.
We do not know love,
because we do not know God.

God is love.
We were made by love
and for love.
But we have turned our backs
on love,
and have become
unloving.

The world has been
disfigured
by our failure to love.
The world will only be
transformed
when all people learn how
to love each other.

Our human love
is limited,
unable to reach
beyond our selves,
our family, our friends.
Our love is feeble,
unable to withstand
the storms of life.
Our love is egocentric,
unable to put others first.

Love requires humility,
mercy, kindness, trust, patience,

perseverance and sacrifice.
Sadly, these noble traits are
Underappreciated
and in short supply
in our troubled world.

Only divine love
allows us to embrace all,
even our enemies.
Peace can only flow
from self-emptying love.

Peace creates unity
and works for the common good.
Faith in God should unite us,
lead us to a peace
rooted in mercy and compassion.
But our flawed faith
divides us,
pits one faith against another,
says my religion is
better than yours,
my religion is
the only true religion.
And so we pray,
and kill . . .
and ignore the poor,
the weak and the suffering.
And cause God to weep.

God is neither Christian,
nor Jewish,
nor Muslim,
nor Buddhist,
nor Hindu.

God is love.
Different religions are
different ways at trying to
understand God.
God is beyond all faiths,
beyond all understanding.

My love for my Christian faith
is enhanced by
my embracing
all religious faith.
Every faith needs
to root out hate
and cultivate
love.

Where there is hatred,
there is the absence of God.
Where there is love,
there is God.

All of Creation

All of creation flows from
a good and loving God;
therefore, all of creation is good.
All of creation is
an expression of God's love.
Because God is the author of all life,
we, along with all of creation,
are brothers and sisters
who are called by God
to be one in cosmic harmony.

All of humanity is connected to God
and created to live in relationship.
All humans were created
to emulate the self-emptying love of God
and to share God's love and mercy
with each other,
especially with those living on
the periphery of society
imprisoned by chronic poverty.

The Poverty of God

No force controls God's action,
which makes God all free.
God does as God wills.

God will give
anything and everything
for us.
This is the poverty of God,
the self-emptying love of God.
God does not accumulate;
God gives all away.

We are called to be like God,
to empty ourselves of everything
but love
and to share that love with others
and all creation
by becoming more and more merciful,
compassionate, forgiving and understanding.

A Question

The radical message
for which Christ died
is dramatically opposed
to our culture
of selfish individualism
and unchecked consumerism.

Should not our Christian faith
compel us,
by means of our transformed hearts,
to live differently
from the rest of our culture,
whose values are rooted
in the material realm
and are far from
the teachings of Christ?

Harmony in Diversity

We are all created
by the Creator,
and so we are all
in relationship with one another.
We are all brothers and sisters,
and to set yourself up
as higher or better
than others is a subtle form
of blasphemy.
We are all connected.
If one amongst us
is diminished,
we are all diminished.

We are one with
all of creation
and the Creator.

We must seek harmony
in diversity
as we rejoice in
our humanness.
The Incarnation compels us
to step to the back
of the bus
and choose to sit
with the poor
and learn to see life
from their point of view
in order to better share
in their struggle
for access to God's gift of
freedom, oneness, and love
that has been denied to them
by virtue of our selfishness.

One Body

The enemy in our battle to overcome
chronic, unjust poverty
is our misguided
spirit of individualism,
our snobbery, apathy,
prejudice and blind unreason.
Though we are many,
we are one body
in the eyes of God,
all animated by
one Spirit.

And as members of one body
we each have a responsibility
for one another.

We cannot separate justice and charity;
they must go together, hand-in-hand,
in order to solve the problem created
by chronic poverty.

Corporal Works of Mercy

We tend to look to governmental polices
to create social change.
Perhaps we should be looking to
the corporal works of mercy
whose roots can be traced to the
25th Chapter of Matthew's Gospel.

You don't change the world
by trying to change the world;
you change the world
by changing yourself.

Change comes from within,
moving from
internal to external.

Slowly, I'm learning
that change is constant.
Moreover, the task of transformation
is extremely difficult,
requiring a great deal of time and dedication.
Every day I must surrender more.

The Common Good

Materialism and consumerism
are stumbling blocks
to entering fully
into the transcendent faith
to which Christ calls us.

Our society glorifies
the amassing
of individual wealth and
an ever-growing
accumulation of goods.

Anything that furthers our goal
of individual material prosperity
is good;
and anything that hinders it
is bad.
Ethics and morality are
not part of the equation.

Economic individualism and
the idea of free competition
without reference to the common good
goes against the spirit of the Gospels.

Every act of love, compassion, and sacrifice
transforms our world in which
hatred, cruelty, and avarice reign
into a new world in which
the kingdom of God blossoms.

Love Is the Key

Jesus asks us
to love as God loves . . .
without counting the cost
or holding anything back.
Love gives all away.
Love frees us
to act for
the good of another
rather than for ourselves.
God's love is
unbiased and all-embracing.
It does not ask
who we are
or how successful
we are at what we do.

Being an instrument of peace
requires us
to embrace
the enemy in pardon.

To give freely
what we have freely received -
namely, God's love -
is the purest form
of evangelization.
Following the example of Christ
will lead us to go poor
among the poor,
without power,
without purse,
without provisions,
with charity and respect
for those we encounter.

We must seek peace
above all else
and then do good
at every opportunity.

If our efforts at sharing God's love
are warmly received, fine;
if not, we should move on.
Our lives are our sermons,
and our preaching
should be
benign and gentle,
spoken with
meekness and humility

Boundless Forgiveness

We must break
the chains
of self-obsession
in order to understand
our absolute dependence
upon God.

Because we are so easily self-deceived,
we have no problem dismissing
the fact that we are sinners
and that we sin daily.
In order to grow closer to God,
we need to awaken a healthy sensitivity
to our own sinfulness.
When we are honest
with ourselves and God,
healing and transformation
can occur.

God's boundless forgiveness
should liberate us
from the chains of sin.

Acts of mercy
take you out of yourself.

Feel mercy. Live mercy.

From Disgrace to Grace

Sin weakens us, then kills us.

Sin erodes the will
and renders it impossible
to stand against
the tyranny of lust
and the allure of sin.

Christ's resurrection
turned disgrace
into grace.

God is part of our nature.
When we turn from God,
our true nature is ruptured.

We cannot find security
in ourselves or in others.

Only a repentant heart
is big enough
to contain God.

Distortion and Lies

Guilt is good.
Shame is bad.

Evil begins with
distortion and lies.

The effect of sin is
it compels us to hide
from God.

Men and Women

Sexism is not God's will.
God intended men and women
to relate to each other in love,
tenderness and equality.
Sin causes sexism.

Temptation

Temptation is not a problem
when I am strong.
But when I am weak
or sad or needy or hurting,
temptation leads me
to feed on my own needs,
give into my own weaknesses.

Temptation has
the presence of grace
within it.

Temptation is not sin,
or a sign
that I am bad.

Without temptation
we will never find
salvation.

We should look at temptation
as an opportunity
to make a choice.

A Broken World

Ours is a broken world
in turmoil.
We need restoration
and wholeness.
We need Christ.

God is
in the midst of evil,
ever ready to redeem it.

God is
constantly revealing
his redemptive power.

If you are a disciple of Christ,
you should be doing
the work of Christ.

Faith should not be
locked up in the mind.

Faith needs to be
lived out
by service
to the will of God.

Doomed

The frenzied pace of life today
easily leaves you feeling
disorientated and unbalanced.
The crush of
time and competition
has nearly squeezed
contemplation
out of existence.
Without regular periods of
stillness and contemplation,
we are doomed.

As we enter
the age of globalization,
human survival
may very well
hinge on the ability of
the world's religions
to enter into a spirit of
genuine dialogue.

We all have a vocation
to contemplation.
Genuine contemplation flows
naturally into action.

Don't Ask

Don't ask God
for more
than you need.
Otherwise, you are asking God
to be a co-conspirator
in stealing from
those in need.

Don't become attached
to externals

Work Force

When our work is rooted in God,
God is rooted in our work.

When our work
is an act of creation,
a material expression
of our spiritual life,
we work in peace
building a better world
for those around us.

A Fiction

Fear is the root
of all violence.

All evil is the result of
our clinging to our egos.

Selfish desire
is the root of
untold suffering in life.

Isolated selfhood
is a fiction.

The notion of having
"rights" is incompatible
with the Christian concept
of "servanthood."

Security, outside of God,
is a dream,
an empty illusion.

A Life of Holiness

God calls us
to a life of holiness.
Does holiness
ever take a holiday?
It does in my case.
I still yield to temptations.
There are temptations
that still seem
beyond my ability to resist.
There are little pockets
of resistance
to holiness in my life
which I have been unable
to surrender.
I am weak.

I keep my unholy behavior hidden.
But God sees, God knows . . .
and God still loves.
But in holding onto these
unholy behaviors
I am keeping myself
from the one thing I really want
the most: God.

How ironic:
I have devoted my life
to fighting the cruel impact
of poverty,
and yet I do almost nothing
to combat my own inner poverty.

Because God is holy,
I want to be holy.
And God's holiness
never takes a holiday.
God is always working
on behalf of my salvation.
And my salvation lies
in forgetting myself
and yielding to God.

Even when I resist God's grace
to overcome temptation,
God's does not look at
my rejection,
but at my heart
which truly wants
to beat with love.

All that I can give God,
who has everything,
is my nothingness,
my emptiness,
my inability to overcome
my own inner poverty.

My Heart's Desire

What is my heart's desire?
It seems to desire so many things,
some good, some bad.
How do I know the difference
between a desire
that is good
and one that is bad?
Maybe I should not think in terms
of good and bad,
but in terms of
healthy and unhealthy.
If the desire is self-centered,
then it is unhealthy,
because it deflects me
from the self-emptying love
that is the one and only path
to God.

Sin is a failure to love;
sin is wanting my own way
instead of God's way.
God's way is paved
with humility.
God gives God away.

A good and healthy desire
is one that longs for God.
When I desire God
more than anything else,
all my other desires
will bow to that
one true, most noble desire:
a desire for God
and God alone.

A desire for God
is nurtured in
stillness and silence.

Stepping Stones to God

Surrender.
Trust.
Humility.
Simplicity.
Authenticity.
Transparency.
Passion.
Commitment.
Compassion.
Mercy.
Purity.
Love.

The Test

The test of seeing the truth
is your willingness and determination
to conform your life to it.
To know Christ
in one thing;
to live as Christ
is something else entirely.

To choose to believe in God
and not live
in accordance
with that belief
is torture.

In This Darkness

We are lost.
All is hopeless.
Look around, the evidence is clear.
War, hatred, violence,
lying, cheating, stealing,
and corruption abound.
Greed and lust have all but become virtues.
There can be no doubt:
we are lost, all is hopeless.
And we are powerless
to change anything.

But in this darkness,
God sheds a light.
What was impossible for us to see —
love, mercy, compassion, kindness, hope —

is possible with God.
God has the infinite power
to change everything.
But we have the on/off switch
to that unlimited power.
And that on/off switch is
surrender and obedience.
To have access to God's power,
we must first surrender our own will
and then submit to the will of God.
The switch is right before or eyes,
but we choose not to see.
We mask our blindness
and hopelessness with
an array of illusions
and deceptions.
And so, the darkness remains
because without God
we are lost and all is hopeless.

Mystical Possibilities

Even the most ordinary moments
of the day
are charged with
mystical possibilities.

To see the mystical
in the ordinary,
we need to pause often
during the day
and be attentive
to what is really happening
all around us
and inside us.

A Choice

We can't escape
conflict
in our lives.
Conflicts are
a part of life.
But we do have
a choice in
how we respond
to a conflict.
And fighting is always
a bad choice.

Conventional Wisdom

You can meet the spirit
of the broken Christ
in the harsh, barren landscape
of unjust poverty,
in dark places
where Christ
still has no home.

Jesus lives outside
the city of conventional thought,
beyond the bounds
of conventional wisdom.

What We Are

The more we worship God
the more we grow in humility.
The more we grow in humility
the more gentle we become.
The more gentle we are
the less aggressive we become.
Stripped of aggression
the more pure we are.
As we grow in purity
the more receptive we are
to the gift of God's spirit.
The more filled we are
with God's spirit
the more loving and compassionate
we become.

Nothing can separate us
from love
if love
is not what
we have
but what
we are.

A Distressing Disguise

God is on a street corner,
at the intersection of everyday life.
If attentive, we can feel
the Divine Presence
in a gentle breeze

as God passes by on the street,
often in a distressing disguise,
hoping for an encounter.
In the ordinary moments of the day,
the extraordinary loving presence
of God
is reaching out
to us.

A Torrent of Trivialities

We do not see or respond to
the unjust suffering of the poor
because we are distracted
by a
torrent of trivialities.
Our lives are swept up
in a perpetual hustle and bustle
as we hurry here and there
striving to make progress
in our endless quest
for more and more.

The Cross and Suffering

Poverty is painful.
But far beneath the surface,
you find the priceless seed of hope.
Not just a fairy tale hope,
but a gritty hope rooted
in total dependency upon God.
As I walked with the poor,

I encountered my own true poverty
and the radical truth of the Gospel:
only empty hands can hold God.

My encounter with
the bloated belly of poverty
revealed the radical nature
of Christianity.

Jesus showed us how to love,
how to love unconditionally
and without limits.
And according to Christ,
how we love the hungry,
the lowly and the lost,
is how we love him;
and how we love Christ
will be the only litmus test
for our entrance into
our heavenly home with God
for all eternity.
And until we enter our eternal home,
we are all homeless,
even if we live in a palace,
because everything on earth is perishable...
except love.

The Incarnation teaches us
that God is humble.
The richness of God is revealed
in the poverty of Christ.
God lives in
our poverty and weakness.
Jesus embraced and loved
the poor and rejected.

For Jesus, the poor are sacraments,
because they offer a direct way
to encounter God.
The poor, broken and rejected
are portals through which
we can enter fully
into the life of Christ.

Christ shows us that mercy
is more than compassion or justice.
Mercy requires us
to become one with the poor and hurting,
to live their misery
as though it were our own.

Christ took his place
with the condemned,
an innocent deliberately allowing
Himself to be arrested.
God's love gives
everything, always.

In Christ, we see a God so generous
he gives himself away out of love.
Christ moved beyond justice to generosity.

My exposure to those saddled
with extreme poverty
uncovered my own clinging selfishness.
I came to see how
consuming more than I needed
was stealing from those in need.

Perhaps St. Francis understood
that it would be hard for him
to feel true compassion
for the poor and the weak
as long as he sought comfort
and required security for himself.

I think St. Francis of Assisi understood
that compassion was far removed
from pity and sympathy,
that compassion grew out of
an awareness of our common humanity.

For St. Francis service to the poor
was not optional...
it was a requirement
for the follower of Christ.

If the Gospel is not about
love and justice,
it has been reduced
to mere sentimentality.
Jesus denounced power
that leads to injustice and poverty;
He asked us to share
what we have with others.
Christianity does not turn away from
the cross and suffering;
it enters it.
Of course, we don't like hearing that!

The Difficult Journey

Everyone experiences heartbreak;
everyone is in need
of tenderness and compassion.
At some point in our lives,
we all have to face
the difficult journey
of coming to terms with feelings
of rejection and humiliation and fear.
These very real and very painful feelings,
in time and in prayer,
become an authentic path
from despair to hope.

Tragedies and disasters become
places of courage, of perseverance,
places where we learn to plumb
the depths of our inner life,
our true essence,
and are able, by God's grace,
to move from rejection and terror
to healing and hope.

Love grows from
that deep-rooted pain
within the universe
where God is present,
and ever-willing to
embrace us and bless us.

The Sacred Energies of Love

True human progress is not about
the survival of the fittest,
which is the case for the animal kingdom.
Human progress requires
converging, uniting.
The more energetically
we are united with others,
the more our different
creative gifts work together
to reach new heights of
human development and consciousness.

We need each other
to become whole.
Human convergence comes
through love.
Love unites
what has become
fragmented and isolated.
And in our unity,
we still keep our individuality,
with each gift of life creating
a beautiful particle
that helps form
the whole of life,
the full body of Christ.
God is unity.

God pulls us out of our isolation
by showering us with the grace
to see that our lives and gifts
must be put to the service of others
and all of creation.

Through acts of sharing and serving
we shall move toward union.
In reaching out to others
we are reaching up to God.

We have not yet begun to tap
the powerful and sacred energies of love,
as Christ asks us to do,
even to the point of loving our enemies.

Through love we shall evolve
to what we were created to be . . .
fully realized children of God
and heirs of heaven,
which can be materialized
right here on earth.

In the Eyes of Jesus

Human need
—be it physical, emotional, spiritual or social—
was Jesus' reason for being.
Christ wants us to respond to
the suffering that torments the poor.
Jesus wants us to create a society
where human lives are
dignified with justice,
uplifted in compassion,
and nurtured by peace.

The ever-increasing world of violence
that threatens us all can only be defeated by love,
by the reaching out of a hand
in a moment of darkness.

Compassion is the most effective response
to hatred and violence.
Because of the birth, life, death
and resurrection of Jesus Christ,
we know that every birth, every life,
and every death matters to God . . .
and matters to us.

Christ always approached people
in a gentle, humble manner,
seeking only to refresh them
with a tender touch, a kind word.
He always personified the love
to which he called others.
He gave himself fully to everyone.
He saw every one as a brother and sister,
a child of God.
He broke down the walls
that separate humans from each other.

If we are to be the incarnate body of Christ
we too must love,
must give ourselves away,
must be with the poor.
Our individual welfare
cannot be separated from
the welfare of those around us.

True compassion stems from
fellowship and interdependence.
The God whom Jesus reveals
in not a God consumed with power,
but a God interested in relationships
of caring fidelity,
a God who is in solidarity
with the most vulnerable and most needy.

Jesus gives and forgives.
When we walk with Jesus,
God's generosity is guaranteed,
making greed and the frenetic pursuit
of acquiring more and more of everything
both inappropriate and unnecessary.

Jesus gives us new marching orders:
love one another.
And in the eyes of Jesus,
a brother or a sister is everyone,
even those who don't look like us,
don't act like us, don't believe like us . . .
and even those who
make us uncomfortable or hate us.

Jesus calls us to
an alternative way of life,
a way which says no to control,
power and domination,
a way which says yes
to trusting in the abundance of God.

Radiant Sweetness

O God how I long for Your
radiant sweetness and abundant goodness
to overflow in my heart.
But I stand in the way
of such a Divine visitation.
My unruly behavior
withdraws the welcome mat
Your extravagant grace seeks.
A stone heart
is hard to enter.

Having felt Grace's embrace
I long to feel it again.
Help me, Lord,
prepare my heart
to receive Her once more.
Peace and purity
are the welcome mat She seeks.

To be pure of heart
requires an undivided heart,
a heart fixed on You
and You alone.
A pure heart
beats with love
for the Other
and every other.
A pure heart
is unsullied
by pride, envy or lust.
A pure heart
only gives
and never takes.
A pure heart
is a humble heart.
A pure heart
is a peaceful heart,
a heart unruffled
by the ups and downs of life.

Peace and purity
are soul mates
living together
in the heavenly chamber
Your never-ending grace
creates within us
as we surrender
more and more of ourselves
to Your all-embracing Love.

The Heart of Darkness

I cannot learn about God.
I can only unlearn
the things that are keeping me
from a full awareness of God.
To find Christ you must make
a pilgrimage to the center of your being,
to the place where
the human and the divine meet.
The key to being a pilgrim
is to remain still interiorly as you journey,
otherwise, you are just a wanderer.
To pray is to embark on
a journey without end—
a journey deep into
the heart of darkness,
of paradox,
of mystery.

The journey to God
is slow.
Each day, we inch our way
along a steep, winding road.
The pace of spiritual transformation
moves about as quickly
as traffic in Los Angeles.

A Prayer for a More Loving Heart

O Most Sacred Heart of Jesus
create in me a pure heart,
a heart that doesn't lust or hate,
a heart that isn't petty, proud, or envious.

O Most Sacred Heart of Jesus
help me purify my polluted heart,
help me soften my hardened heart,
help me warm my frigid heart.

O Most Sacred Heart of Jesus
help me transform my heart
into a heart that beats
more in rhythm with your Sacred Heart.

Jesus my Lord, you are the source
of every blessing and I ask only this:
Let my contrite heart beat with love,
the way your Most Sacred Heart does.

PART THREE

The Fragrant Spirit of Life

*"The whole idea of compassion is based on a keen awareness
of the interdependence of all living beings, we are all part
of one another and all involved in one another."*

—Thomas Merton

I was in Uganda for eleven days in May of 2007, and again in July for 19 days, and once more in January of 2008 for eight days. I was working on a new film, titled The Fragrant Spirit of Life. *All of our time was spent in the massive slums of Kampala and in the IDP (internally displaced persons) camps in the north in an area that has been ravaged by a 20-year-long civil war. What follows is material which I wrote during the trip, much of which ended up in the final draft of the film script.*

A Human Landslide of Misery

We live in a tempestuous, havoc-ridden world.
As Christians, our lives need to be
a healing balm that soothes
the countless wounds and suffering
that torments the lives of so many people.

The violence of war
and the violence of hunger and preventable diseases
need to be embraced
by the peace of Christ.

Within each of us
a war rages.
This is where the first negotiated peace plan
must be implemented.
Once compassion, mercy, peace and love
have been incorporated within ourselves,
we will be able to reach out to
the wounded of the world around us.

The wounded abound in Uganda.
In Uganda, you see
a human landslide of misery,
countless fragile lives
tumbling into despair.

The word "compassion"
comes from two Latin words
which together mean
"to suffer with."

To suffer with someone
you need to go where it hurts,
to places of pain and brokenness,
to places of anguish and misery.

To suffer with someone
you need to enter their weakness,
you need to be vulnerable
with the vulnerable,
powerless with the powerless.

We want to think of ourselves
as compassionate,
yet we want no part of suffering,
want nothing to do with misery,
want to avoid feeling weak and ineffective.

We don't look to enter pain.
We avoid pain at all costs.
We have a ready supply of pain-killers.

Our society is based on competition,
not compassion.
Yet Jesus tells us
to be as compassionate as God.
And God is so compassionate
that the Divine entered into our humanity
and shares in our weakness and suffering.

God, the All-Compassionate, is with us . . .
even in our misery and pain.

And so, we too must enter into
and be with those who are
alone in the world,
alone in their misery and pain,
even if all we can offer
is only our presence.

Give Us This Day Our Daily Bread

Part of the Lord's Prayer
is a request for
the bread we need
to sustain life.
Even though we work
to obtain the bread
we need daily,
our daily bread is
a gift and a grace.
For many people,
having bread every day
is not something
they even have to think about
or pray for:
their cupboards of full.
But for countless millions of people,
having bread every day
is a rarity:
they live with hunger,
with barren cupboards.

Bread is about relationship.
It comes from the earth
and from work
and is for everyone.

The earth produces the grain,
we harvest and produce the bread,
the bread is distributed,
we give thanks for it
and consume it.
Bread is meant to be shared,
to give life to all.

The earth sustains humanity,
she is in a life-giving
relationship
with us.
We need to respect and protect
"our sister, mother earth,"
as St. Francis so poetically called her,
so she can continue
to produce our daily bread,
bread meant to sustain
every one, everywhere.

St. John Chrysostom reminds us
that the sacrament of
'one's neighbor'
cannot be separated from
the sacrament of
'the altar.'

We have an obligation
to share our bread

Change comes slowly:
hunger will not be
wiped out in a heartbeat.
But if more and more people's hearts
beat with love and mercy for the poor,
hunger will slowly disappear.

Each of us might consider
consuming our daily bread
in moderation
so we can share more of it
with those who have none of it.

A Little Piece of Bread

Jesus could have done
anything he wanted,
but chose to be bread
meant to be broken
and handed out to the hungry.
He chose to be a cup of wine
poured out for us.
And Jesus asks us to do the same thing –
to become bread broken
for the nourishment of
the poor and the hungry,
to be like cups poured out
in service to others.

A little piece of bread . . .
a handful of rice . . .
a cup of clean water . . .
an old pair of pants or
frayed shirt of no value . . .
a small coin . . .
a smile or a hug . . .
this is the price of righteousness
in the eyes of God.

We Are One

There is no hot water where we are staying.
A cold shower is hard to get used to.
But it is an easy point of reference
that illustrates the vast difference
between the lives of the truly poor
and our comfortable, pampered lives.
It is our need for
comfort and security
that prevents us
from becoming
one with the poor.

The physical distance between us and
the suffering people of East Africa
may be great,
but in the mind and heart of God
we are one.

We must imitate God
who stoops down in mercy
to touch us.
So, we too must
stoop down in mercy
to touch others . . .
even those who live far away.

A Continuous Trial

Our staying at a place
named after St. Augustine
prompted me to recall
some of the saint's eloquent writing.
In his *Confessions*, he wondered:
"Is not the life of man upon earth a trial,
a continuous trial?"

It certainly is for the poor of Uganda.
And if we are honest,
it's a trial for us too.

St. Augustine said all his hope
rested upon God's great mercy.
Speaking of his own conversion,
he wrote:

"Late have I loved you,
O Beauty ever ancient, ever new,
late have I loved you!
You were within me,
but I was outside,
and it was there
that I searched for you.

In my unloveliness
I plunged into the lovely things
which you created.
You were with me,
but I was not with you.
Created things kept me from you;
yet if they had not been in you
they would not have been at all.

You called, you shouted,
and you broke through my deafness.
You flashed, you shone,
and you dispelled my blindness.
You breathed your fragrance on me;
I drew in breath
and now I pant for you.
I have tasted you;
now I hunger and thirst for more.
You touched me,
and I burned for your peace."

St. Augustine understood that
once we have breathed in
the fragrance of the Lord,
we have no other option but
to share that delicate, intoxicating fragrance
of mercy and love
with those whose lives
are lived on the shadowy and dismal margins,
with those whose days
see no happiness,
with those whose days
end without hope.

Grace Abounds

Pick up a newspaper
any paper, any day,
and you'll find all the proof you need
that evil exists.
It is all around us.
But we are also surrounded by
an even greater reservoir
of goodness.

But the news is so grim,
so filled with hatred, violence and injustice
that you are left with the impression
that humans are basically bad,
even malicious.
Human history is littered
with inhuman, wicked acts,
often on a massive scale,
such as the holocaust
and insane acts of genocide.
And technology has enhanced
our capacity for destruction.
Machine guns and the atomic bomb
make mass killing easy.

No doubt about it:
sin abounds.
But more bountiful
is grace and goodness.
In Uganda you see
the fruits of evil
and the seeds of goodness.

The harsh, chronic poverty
these people endure
does not stem from anything they did.
It grows out of the evil
of our indifference
and the injustice of economic systems
created to make
the rich richer
as it makes
the poor poorer.

Here we see
the utter futility of life;
yet the darkness
is not without hope

In the harsh barren landscape
of northern Uganda,
hospitality is a matter of
mutual survival.
The poor need each other
as much as they need us.
Here, one faces the ultimate reality:
we cannot survive on our own -
we need each other.

In a visit to an Internally Displaced Person camp,
a visitor soon learns
how to focus on
what is truly important
in his or her own life.

The Splendor of Poor Things

We are all poor,
all in need of something
beyond ourselves.
Poverty is our true reality,
which we try to disguise with riches.

Ernesto Cardinal,
the Nicaraguan priest and poet,
said:
"There is a splendor in poor things,
the splendor of what is real."

In Uganda, you see
the splendor of simple, poor things,
things made of clay, straw and plain wood,
homespun things that are
coarse, rough and rudimentary,
yet they reveal the majestic,
naked, splendor of matter.

Ernesto Cardinal reminded us
that it is easy for us
to confuse what we have
with what we are.
We are not more
because we have more.
Nor are we less
if we have less.

St. Francis called poverty
a great treasure.
He possessed nothing but
a pair of sandals, and a sack
that fastened about his waist with a rope.
By owning nothing
he came to possess everything.

Our entire economy is based on greed.
We worship money and property.
We have fallen far from God.
Jesus said we should resist the temptation
of self-preservation and privilege.
He made it perfectly clear
that those who seek self-preservation
are lost.
Jesus gave up everything
and became nothing;
he held nothing back for himself.

Morning Prayer

Birds singing their morning cantatas
mixed with the sounds of
the Muslim call to prayer
and the clanging bells of the churches.

Uganda is waking up.

It will be another long, hard day.
But the day will be sprinkled with
simple blessings and quiet acts of kindness.

As the dawn breaks
you can sense
the natural harmony of life.

You can feebly feel
the pulse of infinite love
beating within
the rhythm of life in Africa.

Here you see
the hands and feet of Jesus
nailed to scrap wood
over and over and over again.

The agony of poverty and violence
cannot still the Spirit
in the soil of the earth,
in the souls of the people.

The fragrant spirit of Life
smiles through
the pain of living
and the mystery of death.

O come,
breathe in the Spirit,
exhale the Love,
give birth to faith and hope.

The hopes of the wonderful people
we are filming
can be easily crushed by
our indifference and inaction
and by our lack of authentic concern
about the abysmal state
of their health care and educational infrastructures.

We can make a difference.
We must make a difference.
And we can do so by
creating bonds of solidarity
with the suffering peoples of Africa.

As we search for
innovative means for development
and for promotion of peace among warring parties,
remember to pray each day for Africa.

Gospel Giving

This is the kind of place
where I come when I really want
to commune with God,
a place where ramshackle huts
are stained glass windows of heaven
which the light of God
pours through.

For me, the far-too-numerous
and massive slums
that dot the landscape of
so many developing nations are
Cathedrals of the Poor,
places so real and raw
that they pulsate
with the presence of God.
In these slums,
you are on holy ground
because Jesus is here
in the form of
people suffering from
hunger and curable diseases.

Christ wants us to live a life
of detachment and expectation.
But we cling to the countless things
we think are important.
We chase after what we don't have;
we lust after what is beyond our reach.
We have turned greed and hoarding
into virtues.
Consumed by our need for
comfort and security,
we have become blinded
to the needs of the poor.
We do not share,
and our selfishness is the cause
of much of the poverty we see.

Economic policies in affluent nations
often have a devastating impact on
destitute people living
in destitute countries,
making basic human dignity

something that is far beyond their reach.
The people in this slum
have no voice, no power, no rights . . .
and no way to make their plight known.

We are driven by economic success.
We worship on the altar of consumerism.
Christ showed us a different way -
a way of simplicity, dependence upon God
and extending good will to others.
Our commodity economy
is not in harmony
with the teachings of Jesus.

We need to share our time,
our treasure, our love
with the chronically poor.
Jesus wants us
to give our lives away.
This is Gospel giving.

Making Sense of Suffering

Whether implicitly or explicitly,
we all seek security and consolation.
Yet even when we find
some level of security,
some degree of consolation,
it isn't enough.
For many, security and consolation
are beyond their reach.
Far beyond.

Jesus claimed
that true security and consolation
could only be found
in God.

In Uganda, seeing so much
intense, unfathomable suffering
shook my notions of security
and unmasked my true
helplessness and inability
to control anything in life.

When you look, really look,
at the suffering on full display in Uganda,
you are forced to clearly see
that life is unfair,
often brutally unfair.

In the midst of so much suffering,
our flimsy ideas of God
are blown to pieces.
God's seeming silence
in the face of
such wide-spread suffering and violence
is baffling.

Yet Jesus is found and encountered
at the foot of the Cross.
The mystery of love
and the mystery of the Cross
are one and the same.

The inflowing of God's love
purges and transforms . . .
and it hurts.

We must die to our
self-centeredness,
must divest our ego
and put on the mind of Christ
and grow in love for all of humanity
and give our lives,
as Jesus gave his life,
so that others may live . . .
even our enemies.

Jesus wants to shatter
our complacency
toward the suffering poor,
wants us to see
and feel their suffering;
he wants us to renounce
our own security
and share our love and material possessions
with those who have nothing.

When we let go of our own security
and put our trust in God alone,
the Kingdom of God
shall expand
and suffering
shall decrease.

A Shimmering Ocean of Love

A small empty begging bowl
holds the great void of life.
Flowing along
with birth and death,
so many people
hauling water and
carrying firewood.
So many people
walking so far
for the basics of life,
being so far
from the elixir of hope.

If the human species
could reach a place
where there was
neither lack nor excess,
we would be entering
a place of inexpressible light,
we would be entering
a place of lasting peace,
we would be entering
a place of immeasurable grace,
we would be entering
the Kingdom of God.

But we seem unable
to discard greed and anger,
unable to live without grasping,
unwilling to embrace the other.
And so, we are unable to sail on
the shimmering ocean of love
that is God.

PART FOUR

The Sun & Moon Over Assisi

*"All praise be yours, my Lord,
through all that you made."*

—St. Francis of Assisi

Making The Fragrant Spirit of Life *left me emotionally exhausted. My three grueling trips to Uganda, broke my heart more than any other place I had been up to that point. Uganda's vast slums are nothing short of a nightmare. The horror of the internally displaced persons camps in the north, where more than 1.5 million people live without water, electricity or enough food for survival, is beyond comprehension. After Uganda, I felt I could not see any more suffering and dying, could not see any more starving children with bloated bellies. I needed a time of renewal; I needed to see beauty.*

My seven-year journey [from 2001–2008] with the poor had been an intense immersion into a hidden world of suffering. Over and over again, I saw Christ nailed to the cross by our inexplicable indifference and apathy. But as I walked down poverty road, I slowly learned about the kind of radical dependency on God which St. Francis of Assisi relied upon.

After filming in so many desperate places, my broken heart had longed to return to Assisi, longed to go home, longed to return to the one place where I could find spiritual refreshment and renewal. Following Francis into the depths of unjust poverty has been a long, lonely journey, during which I've struggled with periods of intense spiritual dryness. Too often, sadly, my longing for God had waned and I thirsted for things beyond God. So, in September of 2008, I headed for Assisi in hopes of renewing my spirit and rededicating my life to God and the poor. I brought cameras on my pilgrimage in order to make a film about St. Francis. Over the next six months, I made four additional, shorter trips to Assisi in order to complete the film. What follows are some of the reflections from the film titled The Loneliness and Longing of St. Francis of Assisi. *The film is a retreat into the mystical heart of St. Francis.*

Hidden and Waiting

A thick blanket of fog
is hiding the sun
and covering Assisi.

The innermost essence of God
is hidden from us,
totally separated from the created world.
We can see only hints of God's love,
which is enduring and incomprehensible.
God is utterly transcendent
and lovingly immanent.

The call to holiness is an invitation
to enter fully into
a committed relationship with God.
As we respond,
God graciously nurtures growth
in the relationship,
by using events, circumstances and people
in our lives as instruments
to hasten a contemplative outlook on life.
Prayer becomes a vital part of our day;
and, in prayer, we encounter more fully
the Author of our life.

This personal encounter with the Creator
slowly transforms us into a Divine likeness,
as it gently erases
all traces
of the un-God-like substance
within us.
In prayer, we unlock
the vault to our deepest self
and allow light to shine on God
who is already abiding
at the very core of our being,
a tangible Presence hidden from us
yet patiently waiting for us.

Icons of Holiness

Somewhere deep inside of each of us,
there is, I believe,
a desire to be holy.
We can quibble about
what being holy means,
but essentially it means
being really, really good . . .
even when no one is watching.
For a Christian,
the essential meaning of holiness
is more precise:
it means being like Christ.
But the manifest goodness
on full display
in the lives of the saints
grows out of love.
Their love of God is
so strong, so deep
that their lives pulsate with
God's love and goodness.

Saints are icons of holiness.
Saints make holiness real;
they show us holiness is possible.
Saints are also fully human.
They make mistakes
and have their share of failures.
They cry and they laugh.
They endure illnesses and disappointments.
They fight long and hard
to overcome doubts and insecurities.
They often experience rejection and scorn
from family and friends.

They struggle with spiritual growth
as they attempt to follow a path
they hope and pray leads to God.
Saints are ordinary people
whose passion to emulate
the self-emptying love of Christ
is extraordinary.
Saints are flesh and blood,
not pious plastic statues.
They are not perfect;
but they allowed the love of Christ
to transform their
weaknesses and imperfections
into something beautiful.

To study the lives of the saints
arouses within us a response,
a desire to imitate real examples of holiness.
The good news is we don't have to be
another St. Francis or another St. Clare.
We simply need to become the saints
we were uniquely created to be.
And in a hundred years,
it will not matter
if we are in a book of "official" saints.
Even today,
there are countless everyday saints
living holy lives of prayer and service
who are virtually invisible.
But God sees them,
sees all of them.
I've met a few of them.
Men and women living the Gospel,
sacrificing everything
as they serve the poor

in Uganda, Peru, Brazil,
Mexico and the Philippines.
They too have inspired me.

Each of us is called
to become a saint
in our own quiet way.

Indispensable

So much of life today
is deeply disturbing,
especially our attitudes toward
poverty and peace.
I can't understand the irony of how
we seek peace by going to war.
Our impulse toward war uncovers
our erroneous belief
that some people are not important,
that some lives,
even the lives of some children
(the children of our enemies)
are expendable.
I can't understand
how we are undisturbed
by the reality
that more than 20,000 children
die every day
from preventable diseases,
most stemming from hunger.
The economic downturn
that is dramatically damaging
the lives of the poor

reveals the utter lack of
moral and ethical constraints
on capitalism and consumerism;
and the unbridled greed of
commodity hucksters
is nothing short of idolatry.
We have become so numbed
by the scope of poverty,
as well as by our own self-interest,
we don't even feel the pain of the other,
don't realize their misery
is also our misery.
As a society we have failed
to understand that our lives
are both interior and relational,
that we are designed for
communion with God and each other.
Our lives have become impoverished
because we do not value simplicity,
do not realize what is truly essential,
and do not reach out to
the chronically poor and rejected.

I think St. Francis came to see clearly
that the fundamental principle of the Gospel
requires that the weakest and least presentable people
are indispensable to the Church,
that the followers of Christ
must be in communion with the poor
and must be willing to love our enemies.
Each of us is wounded in some way;
each of us is an enemy.
We need each other,
and we need God.

Daily Conversion

When St. Francis began to understand
that his life was
a gift of love,
he desired nothing else than
that his life become
a loving gift
to God and others.
This shift in consciousness
did not happen all at once.
The journey from
the assumption of absolute autonomy
and the false egocentric notion
that we are self-sufficient,
to a posture of total surrender to God
and the recognition of
our genuine interconnectedness
with all life
takes time and requires
daily conversion.

Day by day,
step by step,
prayer by prayer
we inch our way
along the Way
back to God,
back to the fullness of life
and love.
But we easily get distracted,
sidetracked by false desires
and empty illusions.
This is why the
discipline of prayer
was important to Francis
and he did not want

to leave it to chance.
He carefully carved out
time alone,
time apart from the roar of the crowd,
time for God alone.

A Culture of Emptiness

Within himself, Francis created
a culture of emptiness,
an empty space for God to fill.
To become empty,
we need to do nothing,
need to press the pause bottom
on our society's addictive need
to be productive,
to always be doing something.

I think we need to create
a culture of emptiness
more than Francis did,
as modern life is
so filled with busyness,
so cluttered with unfiltered information
tirelessly generated by
the media and the internet,
so over-stimulated by
a dizzying array of electronic gadgets,
so pressured by the allure
of nonstop advertising,
and so driven by productiveness,
we are almost incapable of stillness
and can't tolerate silence.
It was in stillness and silence

that Francis forged
his inner cloister of emptiness
and flamed his desire for God.

For Francis, his form of monasticism
had no walls,
for the world was his cloister;
but he was diligent
in periodically retreating
to places of solitude
where he could be renewed
and find a clear sense of direction
for his forays into the wider world
of activity and human commerce.

Beyond All Knowing

God spoke to Francis in the depths of his soul.
And in the silence of his innermost being,
Francis responded.
In time, God, who has no voice,
spoke to Francis in everything.
Francis became a word of God,
echoing all he heard
in the inmost center of his being
during his prolonged periods of contemplation.
Francis' experience of God
went beyond faith,
beyond dogma and symbols.
His experience of God
gave birth to a spontaneous awe
at the sacredness of life, of being.
The invisible Source of Life
touched Francis

and Francis knew
beyond all knowing
that God was real.
And this deep knowing
was beyond explanation,
beyond discussion and debate,
beyond himself.

God wants to touch
each of us in the same way.
God is always reaching out
to us.
Now is the perfect time
to respond
to the perpetual invitation
God is always
sending us.

Summum Bonum

Francis is like an impressionistic painting . . .
different people see
different things in him.

Various aspects of his life
inspire different kinds of responses
in people's lives
when they walk with Francis.

For some, Francis' understanding of
a God-centered peace
is his shining virtue.
Peace and nonviolence were so integral
to Francis' being
that it colored all that he did and said.

Many people admire
Francis' ability to see
the goodness
within people of other faiths,
and his willingness
to engage in
authentic inter-faith dialogue.

For others, Francis' connectedness
to all creation
is truly inspiring
and makes him
the patron saint of ecology.

Others are drawn to Francis
because of his thirst
for silence and solitude.

For some, Francis' ability to combine
contemplation and action
is his greatest accomplishment;
while others love his ability
to remain faithful to the institutional Church
even while disagreeing with it.

Some people are drawn to his simplicity
and his willingness to take God's word literally
and do what it says.

Others greatly admire his fiery passion
to be like Christ
and to live for Christ alone.

For me, all these aspects of St. Francis
have changed me in subtle ways.

But while my encounter with Francis
changed my perspective on
peace and nonviolence,
solitude and silence,
creation and prayer,
it was his love of the poor and poverty itself
which impacted me the most.

Francis led me to the poor,
to the deepest and most profound
levels of poverty imaginable.
It was there that I understood what
radical dependency on God
truly means.
For me the entire Franciscan spirituality
rests on the foundation of poverty.

But voluntary poverty is a source of confusion
for many of those who strive
to follow in
the footsteps of St. Francis.

Even when Franciscans speak
of the poverty of St. Francis
they often speak of it
as an isolated concept
which leads to a certain amount
of vagueness or confusion,
and even to idealizing poverty.
Are we called to live in
abject poverty?
No . . . this is not what Francis wants,
nor is it the ideal way to follow Francis.

Francis' concept of poverty was
interconnected with his concept of God
as the *Summum Bonum,*

or the Supreme Good,
and that Jesus Christ was
the Summum Bonum of God
given to humanity.
Because of his great trust
in the supreme goodness of God,
Francis could give up everything
and depend completely on God
to supply every one of his needs
from God's overflowing goodness.

Francis knew that even in his poverty
he would be very rich
because God
out of Goodness
would supply every one of his needs.
Francis was not interested in appropriating
the things of God for himself.
Francis was focused on expropriation,
letting go of everything for God
who gives it back a hundred times more in return.

Franciscan poverty should not be equated
with the experience of living in desperation.
This is not what Francis or God wants from us.
Francis wants us to let everything go
and joyfully trust that God would supply
every one of our needs.

When Francis faced the end
of his own resources
he was able to see the vastness
of God's unlimited resources.

Francis understood
that a person's spiritual life

will not prosper
without an intense awareness
of their own poverty and emptiness.
All growth begins
in a womb of darkness.

Unity with God,
Francis discovered,
is obtained in only one way:
total surrender.
This is Franciscan poverty.
And this lesson is,
I believe,
best learned
by being one with the poor
and helping to liberate them
from the prison of unjust, immoral poverty
that robs them of their human dignity,
a dignity that flows
from being sons and daughters
of a loving and merciful God.

For St. Francis,
voluntary poverty was a way for him
to always be dependent upon God for everything.
When Francis experienced the
self-emptying love of God,
it awakened his desire
to love God and God alone.
He longed for nothing else
but God.
And most important,
Francis put his full trust
in the grace of God,
the overflowing goodness of God.
Every moment

was pregnant with the grace
to see the boundless love of God
in everyone,
and to return that love
by loving others
and all of creation.

In Francis' eyes,
everything that is good,
every kind gesture,
every act of mercy,
every gentle touch,
every gift of charity,
every embrace of forgiveness,
every moment of peace,
flowed from God.

Moreover, all loneliness,
every disappointment,
the very wounds of rejection,
the bitter sadness of loss,
and the times of suffering
open us
to the transcendent
and allow us
to experience
the hidden closeness
of God.

Without God
Francis knew he was
nothing.
With God
he knew he lacked
nothing.

Grace Is Everywhere

In *The Diary of a Country Priest,*
French novelist Georges Bernanos
has his dying curé exclaim,
"Grace is everywhere."

Every once in a great while,
I'm able to see things
as they truly are,
able to see that grace
indeed seems to be everywhere.
The beauty of catching
a glimpse of abounding grace
is that it makes
my own limitations
feel less severe
and makes God's vastness
appear even greater
than I ever imagined.

The painter Paul Gauguin claimed
he shut his eyes in order to see.
The Sufi mystic Rumi advised
selling your cleverness and buying bewilderment.
What they are saying is
that the heart sees what the eyes can't.
Francis learned that lesson very well,
and was willing to let God
flip his world upside-down.
Conversion is listening to
the events of your life
that change your perspective.
Francis understood he had a need
for an ongoing change of heart,

and ongoing change of perspective
that allowed him to see the way God saw
and allowed him to see grace everywhere.

It was his willingness to be "grasped" by God
that made him unique.
He approached each day with a simple,
very child-like attitude:
God, what do you have in store for me today!
This outlook released him from the
burden of self-groundedness and
into the freedom of being grounded in God,
thus allowing himself to experience
a realignment of his passion,
and a complete re-centering of his affections.

For Francis, conversion was
a liberating experience,
freeing him from the prison of self-rule.

ᵹhe Ꮒuman Ꮧace of Jesus

Saint Francis understood
we all are
the human face of Jesus;
he knew that
all of humanity comprises
the divine face.

God assumed flesh
and was born into a world of
oppression and persecution.
Can we ever grasp the reality
of the divine presence

dwelling in a depraved humanity
and that subsequently
every man, woman and child
is uniquely precious,
equal and blessed,
all brothers and sisters?

Jesus is hungry and naked.
Yet we build and decorate elaborate churches
in His name,
but do not feed or clothe Him.

Every day,
God comes to us
in a distressing disguise,
clothed in the rags
of a tormented and neglected
poor person,
in hopes that the encounter
will provide a place
for healing and hurt to meet,
for grace to overwhelm sin,
for beauty to be restored.

As Fr. Daniel O'Leary writes:
"It takes a great love,
and many deaths,
to transform the eyes
of our souls
so as to see
God's face
in every face.
And inevitably, inexorably,
this love, this hope,
will lead to a crucifixion."

Far and Near

Speaking on behalf of the Lord,
the prophet Isaiah said,
"Hear, you who are far off,
what I have done;
you who are near,
acknowledge my might."

There is a loneliness
to the past and the future.
I am not there;
I am here in the present.
I am far from
who I was in the past
and far from
who I will be in the future.
I am only near myself
in this present moment.

God too is far and near.
Far in the sense
that God leaves us
to ourselves
in order for us
to discover our own hearts
and the heart of God.
Yet God is as near
as the next breath we take,
as near as our very heartbeat.

God is so near
we do not see Her.
God seems so far
because we do not know Him.
Because we do not see or know God
who is so far and so near
we have the anguish of loneliness

at the core of our being.
We know emptiness
not plentitude.
Sadness is always
around the corner;
joy occasionally comes
and quickly goes.

To discover God
in your heart
you must journey beyond
all self-consciousness
to an awareness
of a reality greater
than yourself.
It is a long journey
and a short journey.
And on the journey
we must drop
all notions of God
and all notions of self.
Only then can God
reveal God to you
and reveal you
to yourself.

In loneliness and longing,
we begin our journey to God.
Stripped of everything,
we have nothing,
we take nothing.
Yet our very loneliness
is graced with the possibility
to discover the transcendent.
Even the silence of God
is graced and speaks
of the mystery of God

and God's forgiving nearness,
God's hidden intimacy.
In stillness and silence
we learn about
a love that shares itself,
an overflowing love
that dissolves all alienation
and fills the empty space within us.

God is here in this moment,
waiting with open and outstretched arms,
waiting to embrace and caress you
with endless love.

Kiss this moment
for in it
is perfect joy
and all good.

A Sense of Balance

Life today demands that we be useful.
Many people feel the need
to at least have the appearance
of being hard at work,
even during their personal free time.
It is as if we fear
what lies beyond our usefulness.
Our society views monks and hermits
with suspicion because
a life devoted to seeking God
is incomprehensible
to a materialistic culture.

Our drive for usefulness, for action,

seems to far outweigh our desire to be still.
We want to just plunge immediately
into deep contemplation,
but it doesn't happen.

It takes a lot of time
to still the restless movement within us.
We are doers,
performers who always have
an itch to be acting.
It is hard for us to simply sit
before God and listen.
How can we speak about God,
or share God's love,
when we haven't fully experienced it ourselves?
Francis knew he had to spend time
listening to God
before he could speak
to others about God.

In deep solitude,
Francis transformed his loneliness
into an interior empty space
where he was able to hear
the silent voice of God speaking
about the necessity of love.
Solitude became a place of
engagement with God,
a place of true peace.

In the solitude,
Francis did not so much pray
as he became a prayer.
It was deep, prolonged that he experienced
the spectacular greatness of God,
which he shared with the world.

PART FIVE

The Perfection of Love

"There is in all things visible and invisible wholeness, a
dimmed light, a meek namelessness, a hidden wholeness."

—Thomas Merton

Unambiguous Love and Service

The cost of following Jesus
is nothing less than everything:
one must abandon self in order to imitate
the self-transcendence of the Cross and Resurrection.

The Cross symbolizes
the extremity of helplessness more than
the extremity of suffering.
The Cross rejects power
and accepts surrender.
When we have little or no
worldly power to rely on,
we are able to offer
unambiguous love and service.

The Dynamics of Global Capitalism

Global poverty and
the accelerating destruction
of the environment
are both linked to
the destructive materialism,
selfishness, and competitiveness
that are rooted in
the daily dynamics
of global capitalism.

Turning a Blind Eye

Many people inside and outside
the Church
turn a blind eye
to the fact that Jesus
had a truly revolutionary
political point of view,
and he was all about
ending
the suffering of people
on this planet.

Acting Together

If Jesus was walking
among us in the flesh today,
he would implore us
to act together
to care for the refugees

fleeing the Middle East,
to offer a hand
to undocumented migrants
risking death in the desert
for a chance at life in America,
to end the vast inequalities
on our planet,
and to save the life-support system
of our planet.

Any honest reading of the Gospels
would make that perfectly clear,
which is why the Gospels
are not taken very seriously today.

Jesus Isn't Realistic

In the face an oppressive
and planet-destroying reality,
many Christians just shrug
and say we must "be realistic"
and accommodate the demands
of the market
and not force
strict regulations
on the backs of business
in order to curtail pollution
because this will
reduce profits.

I guess Jesus isn't realistic,
so we don't have to take
him seriously . . .
or so we wish.

But the fact is conversion
is always going to be
a movement away
from selfish ego-centricity
to unconditional self-emptying
love of others,
which is not a journey
we naturally want to embark upon
because it will
cost us everything.

We Are All One Human Family

The poor, the weak,
and the hurting
are God in skin.
To turn your back
on the poor
is to turn your back
on Jesus.
Only with loving eyes
can we see
God's face
in every face,
including our own.

The Gospel compels us
to see
the face of a homeless beggar,
the face of a leper,
the face of a fleeing Syrian refugee,
the face of a garbage scavenger,
the face of an undocumented migrant
as the face of Christ.

When we relieve
the pain and suffering of others,
we make
God's love visible.

We, the people
of all faiths,
are called to be
a people of peace,
people who desire
reconciliation,
people willing to
forgive hurts and heal wounds,
people who strive
to prayerfully live
in harmony with
all of creation.

Loving Service

It is in stillness
that we sense
our emptiness.
In the state of emptiness,
you are better able
to encounter
the fullness of God.

In stillness, we learn
that no one is
self-sufficient.
We need others
and the Other.

Only when I am
vulnerable
is it possible for me
to be
broken
and restored
to the image
of God.

Sanctity is best found
in the depths
of human frailty.

Jesus came
to liberate
not oppress.
Can I do anything
other than
what He did?
Am I a sacrament
of salvation
for my neighbor?
Christ's message
can be reduced to this:
make every stranger,
no matter how poor or dirty,
no matter how weak or unlovable,
your neighbor.
Tough message.
Even tougher
is the fact that Christ
does not want you
to defeat your enemies;
he asks you
to pray for them.

Grace is God's way
of talking to us.
We can best experience grace
and therefore,
hear God
more clearly
when we stop living
for ourselves
and instead
give ourselves
in loving service
to others.
Unfortunately,
it is easier
to be
self-centered
than to be
patient and loving.

Choices

We were made for
growth and creativity.
The creator designed us
to be creators.
What are we creating?
Conflict and war?
Justice and peace?
Those are our basic choices.

Out of Nothing

Out of nothing
comes everything.
Out of darkness
comes light.
Out of desolation
comes consolation.

Shining a Light

Within every one
we meet
there is an
inherent goodness.
It is our duty
to shine a light
on that goodness.

God's Power

To not love your enemies
is to believe
they are beyond
the scope of God's power.

An Obstacle

Every facet of our lives
needs to be permeated
by love
in order to grow
closer to God.
Any portion of our lives
that we have not surrendered
to love,
becomes an obstacle
to reaching God.

God's Tenderness

To live in the reality of God
is to live in
trust, transparency,
and compassion.
To live in the reality of God
is to be embraced
by God's tenderness.

Taking Joy in Forgiveness

We often find it very difficult
to offer forgiveness.
Not so God;
for God,
forgiveness is effortless.
In fact, God takes joy
in forgiveness
because it generates
new life.

The Broken in Body and Spirit

The Gospels make it abundantly clear
that God is on the side of
the poor, the broken in body and spirit,
and the outcasts of society,
the lepers, the prostitutes, the orphans . . .
and today, we must add the addicted.
Did you bring good news
to the poor today?

In My Brokenness

At the heart of every life there is
a deep, mysterious pain.
No one can avoid it or cure it.
My faith tells me
that God loves me
in my brokenness.
And that God loves me
fully and unconditionally,
without a hint of reservation,
even in my darkest, most sinful,
most unloving moments.
God does not demand perfection;
God gives love.
The essence of faith is trust . . .
trusting in God's
undivided, unmerited love.

Only One Question

Often in life,
we make a complete change
of direction
and boldly head off
into unknown territory.
When I was working
in network television,
cranking out mindless soap operas,
I could never have imagined
I would travel the world
making documentary films
on global poverty or
end up living in Haiti,
caring for five dozen
abandoned kids.

I think I'm on the road
God wants me to be on.
I guess the actual road
we take
isn't really all that important,
as long as it leads us
back to God.
Returning to God
is the destination of
our life's journey.
There are so many routes
we can take.
And there are lots of roads
that take us the wrong way
and we get lost.
The journey is replete
with dead ends, detours,

and road blocks.
Sometimes, U-turns
are essential.

Today it seems the path to God
is the road less traveled.
Our society is headed
in the wrong direction.
The ways of the Lord
do not seem to be our ways.
We want to consume
more and more.
We want to succeed in business,
no matter the cost.
We ignore the poor.
We want to wage war.
We hardly live as if
we believe in God.

Charles de Foucauld,
the Christian contemplative and mystic
who lived among
the Tuareg people of Algeria, said,
"As soon as I believed there was a God,
I understood that I could not do
anything other than live for him."
If a poll were conducted
that asked the question
"Who or what do you live for?"
I would bet God would be
near the bottom of the list of answers.
And the reason God would poll so low
is that there is a rupture
between what we believe
and how we act.

It puzzles me
how so many Christians
(including me, a good deal of the time)
live lives that bear
no resemblance
to the life of Christ.
Am I a follower of Christ
or a follower of the latest trend in society?

While we busy ourselves
striving for power
and trying to control events
and even people,
the Gospel perpetually proclaims
a far different approach to life:
God has created us to live
a life of dependence and receptivity,
and our acceptance of
that spiritual reality
is required for true human growth
and fulfillment.

To live the Gospel forces us
to live with contradiction—
for the Gospel requires a faith
which believes that
when one has nothing,
one has everything.
Moreover, it asks us
to count poverty
as riches
and humiliation
as an honor.
Of course, this sounds like
utter nonsense,
even to those who profess

to be followers of Christ.

But even a casual reading of the Gospel
reveals that Jesus denounced
power, injustice and poverty.
Christ moved beyond justice
to generosity.
If the Gospel is not about
love and justice,
it has been reduced to
mere sentimentality.
And so, for followers of Christ,
service to the poor and lowly
is not optional...
it is a requirement.
Christ gave us
an understanding of divine justice
that is based on divine mercy.
When we turn our back
on the poor,
we are turning our back
on Jesus.

We want to be served.
Jesus wanted to serve.

We want a cozy Jesus;
but Jesus is far from cozy.
The core of Christianity
is about the Cross, suffering,
renunciation, and sharing
what we have with others.
Yet, our society proclaims
a dramatically different message.
It tells us to grab all we can,
to live for ourselves.

It urges us to be independent,
to deny the interdependence
of all living beings
and to ignore that we are
dependent upon God
for every breath we take.

When Charles de Foucauld understood
he could not do anything other
than to live for God,
he caught a glimpse of
the ultimate truth:
human beings by their nature
are compelled to turn toward God
and eventually devote themselves
totally to God.

The great Sufi mystic and poet Rumi
wrote about how
the "profession of God's unity"
needs to reverberate
through all our thoughts and actions.

The prophet Mohammed said,
"Knowledge without works
is like a tree without fruit."

When our hearts are enlightened
by grace
to the "knowledge"
or awareness of God,
we are driven to apply
this interior knowledge
to our everyday exterior life.

What the mystics
and saints of all faiths
came to realize is
that to enter the heart of God
is to enter a school of love.
When we first experience
God's love,
our spirits are dazzled by delight
and we are left
in a state of bewilderment.
In the wake of the experience
of all our previous thoughts and ideas
being overturned,
we realize
that without love
we are naught.
And love must be shared,
must be given away.

There are so many paths
we can take in life.
No matter what path we choose,
the path needs to be paved
with love
in order for it
to lead us back to God.
Where there is love . . .
there is God.
Everything we do
needs to be done in love.
And that means
we must continually strive
to root out all anger and violence
from our lives.

Jesus said, "Peace be with you,"
because he knew that God
was a God of peace,
and that perfect peace
is the fruit of perfect love.
What God had in mind
when he created each of us
is that we would attain
the perfection of love,
becoming instruments of peace,
mercy, kindness, and compassion.

At the end of
our individual journeys,
God will ask us
only one question:
In the adventure of your life,
did you learn to love?

I fear I would have to answer,
"Not really."

PART SIX

Thoughts of a Blind Beggar

*"The deepest wisdom man can attain is to know
that his destiny is to aid and serve."*

—Abraham Joshua Heschel

This section of the book contains material from my book *Thoughts of a Blind Beggar,* which was published by Orbis Books in 2007. The book is now out of print. I selected a few pages of reflections from the book that I like and wanted to give new life.

฿eart and Soul

Transformation is not possible
where we,
not God,
are secretly in control,
cavalierly pretending we "know-it-all."

By recognizing my weakness
I become strong.

God is humble.
God lives in our poverty and weakness.

Simplicity safeguards the spirit
from distractions and leads it to God.

Love and trust are the heart and soul of simplicity.

Uncovered

You can't be converted
without becoming naked
and seeing clearly
all your faults and weaknesses.

Passion is an expression of
love or hunger.

Do not judge others;
instead, live with God.

The closer you come to God
the more compassion you will have
for your neighbor.

Making Headway

Stop measuring your progress.
In fact, let go of the idea of "progress."

Look for "moments" of prayer.

Prayer helps us remember
that our life is a journey
to God.

Growth in purity is linked
to increasing our ability
to establish and maintain
solitude of soul for God alone.

Radiant Love

God speaks to us even in the smallest
and most ordinary events of daily life.

God's love does not shout, it whispers.

Be still and hear God whisper
soft words of fondest love.

Listen...don't think.

Love should radiate, not dominate.

Conflict Resolution

Prayer is hanging on to God,
stubbornly clinging to God.

Beg for the grace of prayer.

The universal lack of an interior life
is a key element behind the rash
of violent political and religious conflicts
that plague so many nations.

You Are What You Eat

Prayer is about loving and being loved.

Simplicity is in harmony with contemplation.

Prayer deepens with purification of faults.

You grow into what you dwell upon.

Progress along the spiritual path
is fueled by desire.

Doing What You Love

Salvation is discovering
who you really are.

The surest way to death
is not to discover
what you love.

Knowing what you love
helps you reorder your life
in order to do what you love.
When you are doing what you love,
you become love.

The Bottom Line

Prayer stimulates a mindfulness of God,
which in turn stimulates acts of love and mercy.

Love is service.
It is the emptying of self.
It is losing in order to find.

Acknowledging my own weakness
increases my ability
to be more merciful towards others.

The Christian life can be reduced to this:
live the beatitudes.

Shut Up

If Christ is the center of my life,
then I am not.
This is good.

Tell your ego to shut up.

Let yourself be loved;
let yourself be acted upon by God.

Contentment is the daughter of simplification.

Faith in Christ means I allow my life
to be illuminated and sustained by His life.

Not Fickle

My awareness of God's mysterious presence
within me
helps me become more aware
of the same presence within others.

To love others as Jesus loves them
is an extremely difficult,
if not impossible,
task, yet it must be
our primary goal as Christians.

The key to attaining happiness
is to give it away.
But we love hanging onto
what we've got.

Divine love is not fickle.
It has only one desire:
total self-giving.

Happiness grows only in the garden
of unconditional love.

Charity is the art of knowing
how to do the will of God.

The Surest Way

The longer I walk with the poor
and with Jesus-
the more I see the need to put to death
the idea of my own self-sufficiency.

To think of myself as separate
from God and all of creation
is an illusion.

To be in communion with those who are suffering
is the surest way to chip away
at the notion you are a separate self,
detached from the rest of creation.

Letting go of my life
is the surest way
to a life of abundance.

Eternal life is not something that happens
in the future:
it is now.

A Different Point of View

The infancy story of Christ
tells us we can have hope and joy,
can overcome our immense loneliness
and can find
unity, integration, solidarity
and reconciliation of all,
with all.

At its root, there is only one reason
for the existence of poverty:
selfishness, which is a manifestation of
a lack of authentic love.

Sadly, we tend to think of the homeless
as social nuisances.
Jesus had a different point of view
and suggested that the poor
are pathways to God.

By serving the poor
we are not only practicing Christian charity,
we are also reforming ourselves.

We don't have to solve
all the problems for the poor;
just being with them
goes a long way toward
lightening their burden.

The witness of love
lived in voluntary poverty
has the peaceful power
to change hearts.

Make Believe Time

God is present and living in the world.
Better to see the Lord here on earth
then to try to penetrate the mysteries
of another world beyond death.

Stop brooding over the incomprehensible
which is beyond the power of understanding.

Punctuate your day with thoughts of God,
recalling God's unselfish,
self-giving love for us.

Recapture your childhood faculty
for make-believe.
Let go of your sophisticated ways.

Stand before God in a stance of conversion.

Handle with Care

Every moment is a moment of grace—
if my eyes and heart are open.

Handle all life,
and every moment of your life,
with care, respect and love.

Morning prayer is the most important prayer of the day...
it sets the tone for all that will follow.

Planting a Seed

God is near.
God is warm.
God is tender.
It is time we stress these softer
attributes of God.

Plant a seed of gratefulness in your heart,
so that day by day
you grow more thankful to God
for the overflowing goodness and mercy
God has lavished upon you.

Only when I am able to see
my own unholiness
can I begin to see
the sacredness of all creation.

A Scared Space

We can turn any space
into a sacred space.
A bedroom corner
can be a basilica,
a portal into
the mystery and meaning of life.

Waiting, waiting, waiting.
Our spiritual lives are a vigil
of waiting.
We wait with hope
for the advent of God.

Yet as we wait for God,
God is already here with us.
And we are with God,
yet not fully so,
and so, we wait,
living with paradox and expectancy.

Spiritual transformation
never ends . . . it is always new,
forever beginning.

The Everyday Stuff of Life

We all love big, flashy miracles,
but when you see the wonder,
the miracle within,
all of life becomes miraculous,
and the everyday stuff of life—

the ordinary and mundane tasks of living—
are transformed into moments
of beauty and joy.

The gift of self-abandonment allows us
to live fully in the present moment.

We are the measure of
our possibilities and limitations.
God has no
restrictions or limitations.

Ḩiding in the Shadows

My wealth lies in God's love for me;
my poverty lies in my lack of love for God.

The hunger for God can never be satisfied.
The more we taste of God,
the more intense our hunger becomes.
The journey to God is eternal.
The more we experience,
the more there is to experience.
God is inexhaustible,
and far beyond our capacity to apprehend.

Recognizing God in a burning bush would easy;
seeing God in the shadows is very hard.
For the most part, God hides in the shadows,
and rarely appears in a burning bush.
We banish the shadows
with the bright lights
of empty diversions.

The Streets of Life

The spiritual life does not lift us
above the human condition —
its misery, problems, confrontations,
pain and difficulties.
Spiritual life plunges us
deeply
into our humanity.
It would be nice
to sit in church all day,
hands clasped in prayer,
drinking the ecstasy of the Lord.
But that is unrealistic;
we must enter into the marketplace,
walk the alleys of commerce.
We must help each other
out of the ditches into which we fall.
In the streets of life
we encounter God.
Everything human is divine.

A Singing Cloud

All of creation sings
of the splendor of God.
Today I heard
a cloud sing
as the rays of the sun
cut through it.

Along the spiritual path,
the concept of
reward and punishment
must evolve (or dissolve)
into the concept of
wholeness and division.

The Sunrise of the Soul

The frenzied pace of life today
easily leaves you feeling
disorientated and unbalanced.
The crush of time and competition
has nearly squeezed contemplation
out of existence.
Without regular periods of
stillness and contemplation,
we are doomed.

As we enter the age of globalization,
human survival may very well
hinge on the ability of
the world's religions
to enter into a spirit of
genuine dialogue.

We all have a vocation
to contemplation.
Genuine contemplation flows
naturally into action.

Transfigured by Grace

Christ is radically present
in the entire universe
as its ultimate fulfillment.

In creation we contemplate
a manifestation of God's face,
of God's presence—
and our souls are set a fire
with charity
for all of creation,
leading us to embrace
the whole world,
a world deformed by sin,
yet transfigured by grace.

A Humble Disguise

Through creation we can pick up
the footprint of God.

Beauty is a vestige of God.
God made the flower
and your reaction to it
picks up a vestige of God.

Oh, how we long to find God
in some moment of spiritual ecstasy,
looking for the Divine in some spectacular
or extra-ordinary event.
Yet God comes to us,
if we are to believe
—fully believe—
what scripture says,
in a humble disguise,

in unexpected places.
God comes to us
poor, hungry, thirsty,
diseased, imprisoned, alone, and lonely.
God comes to us in a homeless old woman
forced to use a public street for a toilet.
God comes to us in people, places, and ways
that make it difficult for us
to see Him or receive Him.
We don't find God
where we expect or want to find Him.

I saw Jesus over and over again
in a leprosarium in Manaus, Brazil.

God's Healing Hands

The real sin hidden within
the plague of global poverty
where millions upon millions are suffering
from hunger and curable disease
is our inexplicable indifference,
our complicity and complacency.
The Gospel tells us we must not look away
from the suffering, must not ignore the poor.
The Gospel tells is tells us to embrace
the suffering and the weak,
to be God's healing hands.

According to Jesus,
you cannot honor God
and dishonor the poor at the same time,
nor can you wage war
and worship God at the same time.

Watch how a person treats
the poor and the hungry,
the sick and the stranger,
and you will know that person's view of life.

You can measure the value of spiritual experiences
by the extent to which
they returned the individual to the physical world
with an enhanced sense
of responsibilities to others.

Empty Hands

The world demands more and more from us.
God only asks for empty hands.

I missed yesterday.
I was too busy to see it.

God resides in the beyond
that lies within.

We find it more comfortable to put limits on God,
and in doing so we create
a spiritual poverty within us.

Allow God to turn your life
upside-down and inside-out.
Allow God to topple your expectations.
Journey beyond comfort.
Pursue true knowledge.

A Light in the Darkness

My anguish, my fear, my temptations
can become a path to God
if I acknowledge my littleness, my weakness
and transform them into a trust
that God alone can bring
light into my darkness
if I abandon myself completely
and take refuge in God's love.

When we embark on an inward journey
we eventually arrive at a place
of keen awareness of our own
powerlessness and hopelessness,
and, like Christ,
must yield to the mercy of God.

The Plague of Consumerism

Relinquishing the possessions of the ego
we all amass inside ourselves
is the most demanding form of poverty.

Simplicity immunizes you from
the plague of consumerism.

Through simplicity we learn that self-denial
paradoxically leads to true self-fulfillment.
Simplicity allows us to hold the interests
of others above our self-interest.
Real simplicity is true freedom.

Doing What You Love

Entering into solitude with the idea
of affirming ourselves,
separating oneself from others,
even interiorly,
in order to be different,
or by intensifying one's individual self-awareness
is not in harmony with
the purity required for spiritual growth.

For the Christian, pure solitude is a place
of self-emptying
in order to experience union with Christ;
in the interior abyss we become detached
from our petty false self
and open ourselves up
to the vastness of the Infinite.

A Deep Need

All addictions mask a craving
to be loved
and express a need
for acceptance or power.

The emptiness we feel
stems from not realizing
we are made for communion with God.
If we are not growing towards unity with God,
then we are growing apart from God.
We need to bring to Christ what we are,
so that in time we become what He is.

We all crave to be on the receiving end of
a gift of love;
but our very craving masks a deeper,
more profound human need:
to give love.

Breaking the bondage of egoism
is the toughest task in life.
Liberation is difficult and painful.

A Place to Sleep

Jesus embraced simplicity, poverty and humility.
What do we embrace?

God hides in a piece of broken bread
and in the broken life of a slum-dweller.

The life of Christ makes it clear
that God choose humility over majesty,
that infinity dwells in the finite.

While God's love embraces all people,
God has clearly demonstrated deep concern
for the poor and the needy,
the helpless and the oppressed.
God demands that we side with the poor,
the powerless and victims of injustice.
To walk with the poor
is to be in harmony with the will of God.

Justice requires that all people
have a place to sleep, enough food to eat,
and work that makes them feel worthwhile.

You First

Jesus instructed us
to never think of ourselves
as more important than others,
to never put ourselves before anyone.
His message is clear:
think little of yourself
and be happy that others
do not consider you very important.

Moreover, Jesus asks us to stop struggling
to control events for your own benefit,
and instead try to be a servant to others.
Sadly, I find it easy to ignore His advice.

Self-importance fosters an addiction
to and craving for human respect.

I am the source of my own misery.
As my ego decreases,
happiness and peace increases.

It is impossible to be filled
with the spirit of God
if we are filled with ourselves.
Surrender precedes the indwelling
presence of the Spirit.

A Hard Time

God's love and mercy are far greater
than my countless infidelities
and my inability to totally
surrender my will.
Thank God.

God grant me the grace
to truly feel my intrinsic poverty.

We have become so separated
from the poor and the suffering
that we have lost the chance
to find true fulfillment by giving of ourselves.

As long as I enjoy comfort
and require security,
I will have a hard time
feeling true compassion
for the poor and the weak.

The Cloud of Unknowing

My greatest challenge:
make the invisible reality of God visible.

The widespread suffering caused by injustice
is ample proof that most people
do not really believe in God.
True belief in God would demand
we end all suffering caused by injustice.

Wisdom is being comfortable in the midst
of uncertainty and change;
it is content under the cloud of unknowing.

The pursuit of power and independence
is counterproductive to the spiritual growth,
unless it is able to be transformed into love.

Love is the ultimate vulnerability.

Knowledge is useless without love.

The Imitation of Christ

Weary are my days
when I crave God and resist God
at the same time...
which I do nearly every day.

All God wants is a surrendered heart.

The road to God takes us through
conversion, contrition and communion.
And it does so on a daily basis.

The desire to imitate Christ
is the first step in actually doing so.

Can I trace Christ-like patterns in my life?

How quickly our "hosannas" of Palm Sunday
turn into Good Friday cries
of "Crucify him."

Our sins shout, "Crucify him."

Awake and Aware

The love of God leads us somewhere -
we just do not know where.
We have no choice
but to follow God into the unknown.

Give your heart eyes,
alert eyes,
eyes wide open to the presence of God.

The unhealthy habits of our hearts
hinder our ability to embrace God.

The biggest obstacle to prayer
is the way we pray,
trying to verbalize everything.
Effective prayer goes beyond words and images;
it requires a complete awareness of the present moment.

Stay awake and aware...
open to the present moment.

Little Gestures

Love is for giving and forgiving.

Our greatest violation of poverty
is to hold the good God gives -
goodness has to flow.

Love is made visible
in the little gestures of our lives.

Acts of charity are the wings of Love.

All good must be given back to God.

Meek and Humble

Humility is the cornerstone of repentance.
Sadly, humility's stock has declined in our time.
Instead, we value a sense of pride,
a sense of self-glorification,
a sense of self-righteousness.
Today, many people view humility
as a sign of weakness.
How easily we forget the words of Christ:
"Learn from Me for I am meek and humble in heart."

Repentance, deeply rooted in humility,
is a return to the right order of things.
Repentance is the path out of exile.

Repentance is more than "pleading guilty"
to transgressions.
Repentance needs to acknowledge
our alienation from God,
our failure to enter fully into the joy
of communion with the Divine.
Repentance is not merely a response
to a spiritual indictment;
it must also be a response to the fact
that we have strayed from the glory of God.

Authentic Transformation

Outside the inevitable suffering
caused by death and accidents,
most suffering bubbles up out of
our craving for transitory things
and our worldly attachments.

It is easy to become attached
to the kind of secure certainty
peddled by religious fundamentalism.
But this kind of "knowing"
is a road block to true knowing.
Clinging to the comfort of certainty
is just as bad as all our temporal attachments.

It is difficult for God's Word to enter
our inner temple
because its entrance is blocked
by our endless array of attachments.
In order to be heard,
God requires silence and detachment from us.

Without daily contemplative silence
it is impossible to have
a true encounter with God's Word within us,
where authentic transformation begins.

Empty Pleasures

To be a saint is to be fully human.
And fully aware that true happiness
comes from God alone.

Each day I must confront
the countless desires
that rise up within me.
And each day I must admit
that I am powerless
to satisfy those desires.

Moreover, I must focus on the fact
that all desires are fulfilled
only in God.
The deepest and most essential longing we have,
no matter how hidden or misunderstood,
is a longing for God.
That longing, that call to holiness,
is woven into the fabric of our existence.
Each day, I need to affirm
my dependence on God alone.

Unhealthy desires are extinguished by humility.
See your nothingness; forget your self
and live for God and your neighbor.

Oh God, help me stop
my restless searching
for empty pleasures,
which even when satisfied
leave me feeling unsatisfied,
leave me with a void
that can only be filled by You.

Wings

The hunger for God is insatiable.
The more the soul glimpses of God,
the greater the hunger for God.

To be in love is to be attentive
to the object of your love.
Which is why contemplation is vital
if you love God.

Contemplation and compassion
are the wings of Christian life.

The Christian life is composed
of four essential elements:
prayer, community, service and study.

Hidden and Visible

Every day I experience God
both as distant and near,
both hidden and visible.
Each day presents me with opportunities
to grow in awareness of God's presence.
The door to God opens every day.
Each day I must enter the door.
And wait.
The cumulative effect of entering and waiting
allows God to enter
and animate God's presence within me.

A Monet Painting

Think about a painting by Monet.
If you were to get very close to it,
all you would see is random daubs of paint,
imperfect looking individual brush strokes.
Yet when you step back from the canvas,
you see fields of beautiful flowers.

Everyone on earth,
a vast assortment of people,
people of different faiths, different denominations,
are like those imperfect brush strokes
of a Monet painting.

The essence of a Monet painting is its organization,
the combination of hundreds
of individual strokes of paint
working in harmony
to create something beautiful.
And that is what we are called to do:
to work in harmony to bring
hope and healing
to those who are suffering
from the cruel effects
of chronic, unjust poverty.
At the foundation of all our different faiths
is compassion.
We show our love for God
by how we treat
the least of God's children,
no matter their faith.

And this involves more
than giving our spare change.
We need to go out and embrace
the anawim in our midst,
embrace the poorest of the poor,
those completely overwhelmed by want,
without voice or rights
in their surrounding community.

The Jewish Scripture makes it abundantly clear
that to forget the anawim,
is to forget God.

And Jesus made care for the anawim
a litmus test for our love of God.

As Elie Wiesel said:
"When someone suffers,
and it is not you, they come first.
Their suffering gives them priority.
To watch over another who grieves
is more urgent than to think about God."

The Cries of the Poor

We need more than an emotional response
to the plight of the poor,
we need more than feelings of
sorrow and regret.
We need to be moved
by grace
to action.

When we hear the cries
of the oppressed,
the cries of the poor,
we hear the voice of God.

Where there is weakness,
there is God.

We need to ask God
to shatter our complacency,
to strip us of our need
for comfort.

Icon by Lewis Williams

PART SEVEN

Endless Exodus

"We do not fully welcome Christ if we are not ready to welcome the poor person with whom He identified Himself."

—Raniero Cantalamessa, OFM, Cap.

In 2003, I spent a great deal of time walking the migrant trail through Mexico with a priest and theologian from the University of Notre Dame to make a film on the sorrowful plight of the undocumented migrant. The file was titled *Endless Exodus*. I also traveled along through El Salvador. Of all my films, *Endless Exodus* is my personal favorite, mostly because the film taught me much and radically changed my life and the way I viewed all of life.

Endless Exodus is a film about migrants from Mexico and Central America who cross the border and enter California, Arizona, New Mexico, and Texas without any documentation. But the film's focus is not political or social, because the film is really about the spirituality of migration, and our response to the plight of the migrants, many of whom will die trying to cross the desert to get a job nobody really wants.

Endless Exodus is a meditation on migration. The film's scope was rather narrow, unable (and unwilling) to deal with the immense complexity surrounding the problem of illegal immigration. The film simply hopes to shed light on the life of the poor in order to help the viewer better understand why they are forced to leave their homes and countries for a back-breaking, low-paying job in a foreign land whose culture is dramatically different from theirs. But it's not just a film about empathizing with migrants who only want a better life. It's a film that parallels our own spiritual journey through our own desert of doubts and confusions, as the migrants teach us about sacrifice, fearlessness, and dedication in the face of grave circumstances. In this final section of the book I present the spiritual reflections from the film.

After writing a book on St. Francis of Assisi, the focus of my life has been making films about global poverty, and people and organizations dedicated to helping the poor. Endless Exodus is essentially a cinematic meditation on our struggle to understand poverty and Christ's directive that we feed the hungry and be one with the poor. The film strove to capture the face and presence of Christ in the face and presence of the immigrant poor.

A Cruel Killer

The vastness of the desert
is endlessly mysterious,
enveloped in silence.

The Spanish mystic St. John of the Cross
used to say that the desert
was a great training ground for the spirit.
The desert yields precious little
satisfaction for the senses,
and so it is a wonderful teacher
because in the desert we quickly learn
that God alone suffices.
In the silence and solitude of the desert,
we experience our own weakness.
In the desert,
we learn to see that
God is the true fountain
of living water.

Nice thoughts.

But while the desert may have been
a wonderful teacher for St. John of the Cross,
for many this desert
south of the U.S. border
is a cruel killer.

Between 1995 and 2003
when I made my film
Endless Exodus
more than 3,000 immigrants
died trying to cross
the nearly 2,000 mile-long border
between the United States and Mexico.

Migration is part of the very fabric of human life
and has been so throughout human history.
Escaping poverty is one of the main reasons
people migrate.

Globally more than 1.5 billion people
are forced to subsist
on less than a dollar a day.

Every year some six million kids
will die of illnesses that are directly or indirectly
attributable to malnutrition.

Such conditions are what push
people to migrate,
to leave their homes
and even their families behind
for a more dignified life . . .
or even more basically –
a chance to survive.

Migration is now, sadly, is a way of life
for many Mexicans.

Chronic poverty and economic instability forces
many people in Mexico and Central America
to flee hunger in their homeland,
only to encounter sickness in the difficulties of the journey,
imprisonment by the Border Patrol
or, worse, death in the desert;
and those who make it to America
will face estrangement in a new and foreign land.
This is the journey of the undocumented immigrant.
This is also the presence of Christ, who said,
"I was hungry and you fed me."

Slowly over the years
of filming global poverty,
I came to see that
we are all migrants,
struggling to cross
the borders of our own selfishness
in order to be embraced by
the limitless love of God.

Just as Mexican and Central American immigrants
are fleeing the cruel prison
of extreme poverty
in order to find a better life
in a paradise named America,
every day, I must flee
my own self-centeredness,
my own sin,
crossing the desert of self-surrender
so I can enter
a God-centered paradise
of self-giving love.

The words of Psalm 63
take on added meaning
here in the desert,
here in a land
parched, weary and waterless,
and remind me why I am making this film.

Friends told me I shouldn't touch
the subject of illegal immigrants,
saying it was too controversial,
too politically charged.

The story of the migrant
is ripe with biblical symbolism.

The story of the Exodus
and the passion of Christ
are at the core of migrant spirituality.

The story of Exodus is a story of liberation
and journey to the promised land.
The way of the cross is a journey
that reminds us that Jesus
is with us in our most difficult times.
The road to the resurrection
goes through the desert,
through the cross.

The raw and uncompromising vision of Jesus
demands sacrifice.
The prophetic, counter-cultural nature
of his message is too shocking
for us to truly follow.
Many of us, myself included,
want a cozy, neighborly Jesus
who does not demand too much from us,
a Jesus who is content with us
worshipping him without
any sense of sacrifice.

Jesus lived, loved and died for the people
who were despised, marginalized and often hated
in a society intent on destroying them.
These very same people are with us today
and Jesus asks us to wash their feet
and care for them.

We betray Jesus when for the sake of expediency
we are willing to sacrifice justice
and turn our backs on the poor.

When we make space for the newcomer, the alien,
we make space for the son of God to be born again.
Hospitality is the secret to unlocking
the mystery of the Incarnation.

It seems inevitable that some people will get jobs in Cabo,
[a sea-side resort in Mexico]
and some won't,
that some will get water and electricity,
and some won't,
that some people will get across the border
and find a decent job in the United States,
and some won't.
But the Incarnation pushes us
to distrust the inevitable
and to work for a society
in which there is space for all,
in which there is enough
food, water and electricity for all.

The Border We Must Cross

I'm slowly learning to see myself in the migrants.
We are all migrants.
We are all poor.
I need to reject the false security I seek,
and accept my inability to control the future.
Christ asks for conversion every day,
that every day we surrender more of ourselves
to the all-embracing love of God.
This is hard,
very hard indeed.
But it's the border we must cross
to find a better life . . . in God.

Jesus Was a Poor Man

In the face and presence of the poor
we can learn to see the face and presence of Christ.

God is at home among the poor.
Jesus was born in the midst
of their poverty and rejection.

Like the poor and oppressed,
Jesus was despised and rejected.
Like the poor and oppressed,
Jesus was hungry and discouraged.
Jesus did not come as a royal ruler,
as king of the universe.
He was born into poverty
and lived among the poor.
He was an outcast,
living among outcasts,
living among people with no privilege or rights.
His message was so radical,
so unsettling,
he was quickly put to death
for threatening to turn
the established power structure upside down.

Poverty gives birth to hunger and despair.
Poverty means one bad thing after another.
Worse, poverty often also means death.

Death by poverty blasphemes
the reign of life
proclaimed by Christ.

The Kingdom of God

Poverty in Mexico and Central America
is choking people to death.

Jesus established the kingdom of God
based on the Jubilee principles
of the Old Testament.
These principles called for
a political, economic and spiritual revolution
in response to human need.
Jesus intended nothing less
than an actual revolution,
with debts forgiven,
slaves set free,
and land returned to the poor.

Of course, this revolution threatened
the vested interests of the powerful
and therefore put Jesus on the road to Calvary.

A Litmus Test

Welcome to the Tijuana municipal garbage dump,
a nightmarish place
where people are scavenging
through the waste of others for survival.
Families, including kids as young as seven years old,
spend long days picking through the garbage
hunting for scraps of anything reusable
they can find and sell for a few pesos.

Scavenging is a degrading and deadly life.
All manner of ugly diseases are born in this dump.

Infections from cuts received from sharp objects
hidden in the garbage is a constant threat.

A society that turns a blind eye
to such a shameful place
has lost its soul.

The people in this dump
are beyond poor.
The Old Testament had a term
for the poorest of the poor: "anawim."
The anawim were people
completely overwhelmed by want;
they had no voice or rights in
their surrounding community.

Scripture makes it abundantly clear
that to forget the anawim,
is to forget God.
Jesus made care for the anawim
a litmus test for our love of God.

They live off salvaged scraps
of discarded waste.
God wants us to salvage
the discarded scraps of their lives.

We live in a world of cruel poverty,
terrible injustice,
iniquitous inequality.
We need to face this reality,
analyze its causes
and demand structural changes
to eradicate these evils.
We must give hope
to the suffering.

We cannot worship God
and be indifferent to the poor.
Worship without justice and charity
is blasphemous.

We Do Not Care

Poverty will always be with us
because we do not care enough
to eliminate it ...
we're too self-absorbed
to end the suffering of others,
even though the Old and New Testament
repeatedly implore us to do so.

The poor will always be with us
because we do not care.
But God calls us to be
a community of sharing.

It truly cannot be God's will
for so many of our brothers and sisters
to suffer and die
from the cruel effects of chronic poverty.
What is God's will?
Simple: love, mercy,
justice, healing,
peace and forgiveness.

God wills the fullness of life and love
for everyone,
not just a select few.
Jesus came to give good news to the poor,
to offer a communion of love

to every human being.
God wants our help
in creating social and economic justice,
insuring food, shelter, jobs
and humane living conditions for all.

The Road North

It is as if they've been told
the streets in America are paved with gold.
Thousands of footprints in the sand
all headed to the promised land.
Thoughts of a new life aflame their mind
but they will lose more than they will find.

To be a migrant
is to live a life of
fatigue and long journeys.
It is a draining, dreary life,
filled with fear and anxiety.

There are long days in the unforgiving desert
without shelter or shade.
Rattlesnakes haunt their dreams.
It is a life of constant uncertainty
and unbearable physical suffering.

It is a life of being
ignored and scorned.
Migrants are greeted
with deaf ears and hard hearts,
forced to face a wall of ingratitude.

To be a migrant
is to endure a life of

mental anguish,
a life of being unwanted
and unloved.

While they hunt for a better life
they in turn are hunted,
handcuffed and returned
to their prison of poverty.
To be a migrant
often means dying in the desert.

The road north is long and torturous.
You begin by saying goodbye
to everything you love and know:
your family, your home, your friends and neighbors,
your town and church, your dog,
your very history,
the places that nurtured and shaped you,
the mountains you climbed,
the streams where you fished,
the fields where you played,
the tiny store where you bought candy.

Most migrants,
before embarking on this trip into the unknown,
have never been more than fifty miles from home.
With no maps or provisions,
without any tour guides or hotel reservations,
they will simply set out by foot
on a journey that may cover thousands of miles.

If they are lucky,
they'll find their way
to shelters that care
for weary migrants.

The dusty, little town of Altar
is about 100 miles south of
the Arizona border.
Many migrants rest
for a few days in Altar
before beginning the arduous last leg
of their journey through Mexico.

The road north is littered with problems:
the migrant may encounter
police corruption,
beatings, rape,
traffic accidents;
they may be robbed or tossed into jail.
They will feel waves of
hunger, thirst, exhaustion and fear.
They will get sick
and struggle with fever and bouts of diarrhea.
Medical assistance and toilet paper
are luxuries they can't afford.

The journey will take weeks,
even months for some,
with many nights spent in flop house hotels
offering little more than a bed.
Most nights will be spent sleeping
on a piece of cardboard,
or squatting in an abandoned building.
Meals will be found in dumpsters.
Public rest rooms will make them nauseous.
They'll be chased by the police,
bandits and the border patrol.

Whatever money they have will go to the *coyotes*,
the term for the people-smugglers who guide the migrants
through the violent and dangerous canyons

north of the border.
A *coyote* will either lead the migrant to safety
or pull a gun on them, taking what little the migrant has.
And if the migrant makes it across the border,
they get to endure the heat of the desert
where temperatures can hit 120 degrees.
If the heat doesn't kill them, maybe a snake will.
The desert is also home to
scorpions, tarantulas and black widows,
none of whom enjoy visitors.

And avoiding the Border Patrol
is no easy task . . . after all they have
helicopters, planes, jeeps, motorcycles,
huge four-wheel drive SUV's,
heatseeking cameras, night-vision goggles,
and guns . . . all employed to track you down
and send you back.

Migrants who make it to Tijuana,
will find an oasis in the storm of their journey.
Casa Migrante is a shelter for migrants
run by the Scalabrini's,
a religious order of Catholic priests and brothers
that serve the needs of immigrants all around the world.
Casa Migrante offers migrants food and rest
before they attempt to cross the border.

Even if a migrant survives the long journey
and makes across the border,
he might cross paths with
a paramilitary vigilante in Arizona or Texas
and end up with a bullet in his head.

A migrant will endure all of this . . .
for a lousy, demeaning, unfulfilling job

that will pay him squat.
If Sister Death embraces a migrant
during the journey,
at least they will have
nothing more to worry about.

Of all the dangers the migrant faces
during his or her long trek to a better life,
the threat of violence and death
at the hands of vigilantes
troubles me the most,
makes me the saddest.

Violence is sinful.
Non-violence on the other hand
is not a struggle against an enemy
or someone who you think
is threatening your treasured way of life;
it is a struggle with ourselves.
The violence employed by the vigilantes
grows out of their illusions about themselves
and the world in which they live.
The enemy is not the migrant
but the tendency in all of us
to make the other, the foreigner,
different and inferior
and to proclaim ourselves as the norm
and the best example of human behavior.

While the migrant seeks survival,
the vigilante lives in denial,
denial of God,
denial of the equality
with which the world began,
and denial of the brotherhood and sisterhood
that is the point of the Book of Genesis.

We are all God's children,
we are all God's family.
Americans shooting Mexicans
is just another form of domestic violence.

When Did I See You Thirsty?

In the vast desert of pale green shrub and cactus
just north of the border
the only color you will spot is a blue flag
flying atop a 30-foot pole.
Hundreds of these flags
mark the spots where thirsty migrants
can find a splash of clean water.
The water is stored in 25-gallon tanks
by volunteers in hopes of saving
the lives of parched migrants who must endure
temperatures that regularly exceed 110 degrees.

Many people applaud this humanitarian gesture,
offering a humble drink to very thirsty souls.
Yet others condemn it,
saying it only encourages the migrants
by making it easier to cross the deadly desert.

As insane as this might sound,
some people actually put poison in the water
in order to make sure those dying of thirst
don't survive.

Crossing a border illegally is
a relatively minor crime ...
yet many are handed the death penalty
for their misdeed.

A man who volunteers at an organization
that puts water in the desert for the migrants,
told me a story that took my breath away.
The guy came across a young man in the desert.
The migrant was in bad shape,
suffering from an array of small cuts
and on the verge of dehydration.
The man asked the migrant why he would risk death
by crossing the desert.
The answer spoke loudly
to the core of the problem:
"I am already dead –
my going into the desert
gives me a chance to live,
even if I die."

A Migrant Preacher

Christ was a migrant preacher
offering good news to
the lowly, the hurting, the ailing.
He was at home with the exiled;
He sheltered the scorned.
Christ would be in this desert
giving water to those who
are dying of thirst,
giving hope to those who
are thirsting for a better life.

If you are looking for Jesus,
you'll find Him in the midst of those
who are being crucified,
rejected, alienated and oppressed.

Unless we stand shoulder to shoulder
with the poorest of the poor,
we will not find the crucified Christ,
nor experience the richness of His resurrection.

The great Mexican writer Octavio Paz said,
"The Mexican venerates
a bleeding and humiliated Christ
who has been beaten by the soldiers
and condemned by the judges,
because he sees in Him
a transfigured image of his own identity."

Being a migrant is
a dangerous way to live.
Migrants are exposed to
extremes of heat and cold,
of sun and rain,
and days with little or nothing to eat.
They drown in rivers,
freeze in mountains,
dehydrate in the deserts
and get hit by cars or trains.

For the poor,
life is a "via crucis,"
a way of the cross,
a way of daily suffering and death.

For most migrants,
the road to America
is a path to despair.

Leonardo Boff,
the noted theologian from Brazil,
writes in his book,

The Path to Hope:
"God is the God of life,
and always takes the side
of those whose life is threatened
or who are forced to die before their time.
That is what happens with the poor.
Hence the God of liberation
is the God of the poor and the outcast."

It is not enough
to be for the poor,
to stand with them.
We must also
be against their poverty,
a poverty created by
injustice and selfishness.

The migrant's life is
a life of prolonged struggles –
a struggle for survival,
a struggle for dignity,
a struggle for liberty,
a struggle for equality.
The gospel compels us
to share in their struggles,
to share in their liberation.

A Death Sentence

Our borders need to be secure.
But they do not have to be
a border between
life and death.

Illegal immigration should not be
a death sentence.

Thomas Merton said,
"When we extend our hand to the enemy
who is sinking in the abyss,
God reaches out to both of us ..."

When we speak about migrants,
we should let words fly from our mouths
on the gentle yet strong wings of humility.

The incarnation and life and death of Christ
teaches not to place any limits on forgiveness and sharing.

The crucified and transfigured Christ's
message of love
compels us
to judge no one, to exclude no one;
moreover, it requires us
to help others to carry their cross,
fully sharing in their pain and suffering.

Mother Teresa said,
"The poor anywhere in the world
are Christ who suffers.
In them, the Son of God lives and dies.
Through them, God shows his face."

A lot of people are quick
to offer answers to
the problem of illegal immigration.
But few ask the hard questions, like:
Why are people poor?
What are the injustices within our society
that contribute to creating poverty?
What can I do about the injustices I encounter?

Many people are willing to share from their excess,
and for this we must be grateful.
But more is needed:
we must try to eliminate the injustice
that robs the poor of a chance to live.

We are so enticed by the love of power,
we have forgotten the power of love.

Individuals and governments
have the ability to use their power
to either dominate or serve.
We certainly know how
Jesus used his power.

Ferments of Love

Compassion requires a response
to the suffering of others.
Feelings of compassion
must be transformed
into concrete action.

The true moral fiber of any society
is revealed by
how it treats its weakest members.
People on both sides of the border
must all work to create a society
founded on welcome and respect,
embracing the most vulnerable among us.
The global marketplace needs
to create space
for the most vulnerable.

When we are focused solely on
our own needs and desires,
we are unable to hear the cries of the poor,
to see the pain inflicted by acute poverty.

An awareness of suffering and affliction,
both your own and others,
is the key to wisdom.

If we are unable to hear
the powerless voices of the marginalized,
spiritual growth will be impossible.

Forced migration has caused
countless broken relationships,
splintering families.
Children routinely suffer
the debilitating pain of separation.
Fathers, sons and brothers
away for long stretches of time . . .
often forever,
their fate never known.

Disenchantment, despair and death
lingers in the air.

To be in communion with God
compels us to be in communion with the poor,
becoming ferments of love,
striving to alleviate their suffering.

The Great Lonely Void

Migrants cross the desert without any
power, prestige or possessions:
they must trust wholeheartedly in God.
The desert teaches them—and us—to pray.

Jesus also walked the desolate terrain
of the desert . . .
where he battled
despair and doubt.

The desert is a place of
trial, of dryness, of sterility.
For monks, mystics and hermits
down through the centuries,
it's also a place of
communion with God.

For monks and migrants,
the desert is both fascinating and terrifying.
It is the great, lonely void
where humans are brought
face-to-face with themselves,
something we all instinctively dread.

Marginalized in Death

Walking with the migrants
forced me to think more deeply
about the meaning of
Christ's sacrificial love
for the least of his sisters and brothers.

All human need
always moved Christ to action.
For Christ, no sacrifice was too great
to ensure that all human life
was dignified with justice,
uplifted in compassion
and nurtured by peace.

I have no solutions to all the
political and social dilemmas
triggered by undocumented immigration.
All I know is that Jesus
wants us to open our hearts
to those whose only hope
is to risk death in a desert.

Between June 1st and July 14th 2004,
while we were editing *Endless Exodus*,
76 people died in the desert
while trying to enter the US.

On his way to the cross,
Christ did not ask us to rescue him . . .
he invited us to follow him.

Our desire for comfort and certitude
must be surrendered,
so we can enter the experience of vulnerability,
and focus on the realities of hunger, need and prayer.

A Crowded Bus in El Salvador

Jesus said,
"Love one another as I have loved you."
He did not ask us to love HIM
because he loved us.
No.
He tells us to love others
because of his love for us.
What Christ is saying is that
the love of God and the love of neighbor
are inexorably bound together.

We cannot worship God
and ignore people, especially
people who are suffering.

God is within everyone on this
crowded bus in El Salvador.
Yet we are quick to judge and dismiss the poor,
which prevents mercy, compassion
and tenderness from flowing.
Jesus is on the bus,
perhaps even hungry.

God is within everyone
we rub up against every day.

Hard Lessons

Welcome to Skid Row in downtown Los Angeles –
a nightmarish 50 block area
where more than 10,000 homeless people
live in tents, cardboard boxes

and overcrowded missions.
Many of the people living here
are migrants from Mexico and Central America.

While *Endless Exodus* has followed the journey
of the migrants as they try to escape
the prison of poverty,
it has also been about
my sharing the hard lessons
of my spiritual journey
over the past ten years.
When I hear myself talk about
the radical message of the gospel,
I can no longer recognize
the guy who once produced soap operas.

For a very long time,
I was desperately searching for God.
Then in an empty church in Rome,
a moment arose in my soul
in which I felt a movement
that I still cannot describe.
It was impossible to ignore.
I had no choice but to surrender to it.
That mysterious moment
started me on a journey
into the core of the gospel,
into the heart of God.

God was not where God was supposed to be.
God was in a place of silence and surrender,
an unknowable place of deep mystery.
And God became most tangible to me
in the presence of the poor,
in slums of overwhelming want.

In these slums,
I saw the need for me to leave
my beloved valley of desire
and seek an undistracted heart.

The spiritual life is a daily dying
to everything that distracts me from God,
dying to everything that is not God.
For me, there is no better place
to learn how to do that
than in places where the only hope is God,
places where vulnerability and weakness
are ever present.

These have been hard lessons for me,
very hard lessons.
And I am sure things you've heard me
say in these pages
have been hard for you to hear.
But the true radical nature of the gospel
is very hard to hear, let alone follow.

Divine Mercy

Christ gave us an understanding of
divine justice
that is based on
divine mercy.

The heartbeat of the Incarnation is
generosity and love.
In Christ, we see a God so generous
he throws everything away out of love.
Christ moved beyond justice to generosity.

Jesus took pity on the crowd's real need
and called on his disciples to feed them.
Jesus prayed for "daily bread."
Jesus defended those who,
in their hunger,
ate the grain growing
in someone else's field.

Service to the poor and lowly
is not optional...
it is a requirement
for the follower of Christ.
To turn your back on the poor
is to turn your back on Jesus.

If the Gospel is not about
love and justice,
it has been reduced to
mere sentimentality.

Jesus denounced power, injustice and poverty.
The core of Christianity is about the cross,
suffering, renunciation and sharing
what we have with others.
Of course, we don't like
hearing that.

The Living Death of the Cross

In his book, *The Ascent of Mount Carmel*,
the 16th century Spanish mystic,
St. John of the Cross said:
"To come to possess all,
desire the possession of nothing."

His startling words stand in direct opposition
to our American ambition for
power, money, pleasure, glamour, security and
an ever-increasing standard of living.
The saint came to realize that
an unrestrained appetite for these things
fragments the soul,
causing our lives to be
too divided and cluttered
to find the true peace and joy
that can only be found
in loving and serving God above all else.

On the cross, through grace,
reconciliation and union with God
became possible.
St. John of the Cross asks us
to live the Paschal Mystery,
to enter the living death of the cross.
He says,
"The soul must empty itself
of all that is not God
in order to go to God."

The detached heart knows the fullness
of peace, joy and freedom,
and sees the face of God
illuminated in all of creation.

Those who struggle for their daily
bread can offer great insight
to those of us who struggle
to go deeper into our spiritual lives.

The road to mystical consciousness
is paved with an acceptance of our
natural state of exodus,

acceptance of the reality of human misery,
acceptance of our limitations and fragility.
The poor know about these things.
And the humanity of Christ illuminated
the vulnerable character of human nature.

As I made this film, I came to see that
an awareness of oppression
and a struggle for justice
are integral to genuine mysticism.

The all-embracing Christ
invites us to be with Him,
so that He,
through us,
can be with all people.

We are all migrants.
As people of faith,
we are migrants
going from sin to grace,
from earth to heaven,
from death to life.
Our migration is grounded in
our belief that God
first migrated to us
in the person of Jesus
and through him
we are called to migrate to God.

If migration worked itself
into the self-definition of all human beings
we would not be as threatened
by migrants as we often are;
instead, we would see in them
not only a reflection of ourselves
but Christ who loves us.

Day of Atonement

Almost a year ago, in August of 2003,
as I drove across the Arizona desert
heading for Mexico . . .
I was really ignorant about the plight of the migrants.
Before crossing the border,
I had no idea where the journey would take me.

This film taught me one essential lesson:
we must not judge others.
It is so easy to condemn
the migrant sneaking across the border,
but we must resist the temptation
to judge them or hold ourselves up
as better than them.

We are all brothers and sisters.
We are all connected.
The ideal of compassion
is based on a keen awareness
of the interdependence of all living things.

And we live in a world that is filled with pain.
The planet is covered with people
who are overwhelmed by suffering.
Wars, famines, economic injustice, diseases
and natural disasters
are killing people every day.
I've seen a little of it.
We are impotent when it comes
to making the pain go away.

Life is hard and messy and painful.
Hurt abounds and hope is in short supply.

Jesus did not clean up every mess
or relieve all the pain he encountered.
Jesus simply told us to take the pain
and the mess of our lives
and place them before God.
Even then, the answers to the riddles of our lives
are not always perceivable or even obtainable.
Jesus teaches us to live with the questions,
to live with the pain.
Peace, He suggests, is found in faith.
God is bigger than we are;
and we, in our weakness,
need to lean on the strong arm of God.
Cures and answers may not come to light,
but faith, hope and love changes
who we are and how we deal with
the messiness and pain of life.

Our spiritual life will not prosper
without an intense awareness
of our own poverty and emptiness.
The source of wisdom
is hidden in the shadows of life.

Endless Exodus was been about journeys,
the physical journey of the migrant,
as well as our and their spiritual journeys.
In his last book, *The Asian Journal*,
Thomas Merton reminds us,
"Our real journey in life is interior;
it is a matter of growth, deepening, and
an ever-greater surrender
to the creative action of love and grace."

I would like to end with a prayer
Jewish people pray
during the Day of Atonement,

the holiest day of the Jewish year
marked by a 24-hour fast
during which all work and business
are forbidden except God's business:
"For the injustices we condoned
and the times we kept silent
and our unwillingness to learn
and our self-pride,
O God forgive us,
pardon us,
and grant us Atonement."

Closing Prayers

"Strip your prayer, simplify, de-intellectualize. Reach God not through understanding but love."

—CARLO CARRETTO

A Fresh Beginning

As each new day dawns,
God's light gives us
a renewed pledge
of God's love,
a fresh beginning
that is pure gift,
a gift meant to be given away
during the day.

In the silence
between night and day,
we feel God's
grace and peace
and are commissioned
to become instruments
of that very same grace and peace.
In the splendor of new light,
God's love and mercy
are revealed.

O God help me to see
the radiance of Your light
and show me this day
how to be a servant of Your peace.
Help me, O God, to share
the delicate, intoxicating fragrance
of Your mercy and love
with those whose lives
are lived on the shadowy
and dismal margins,
with those whose days
see no happiness,
with those whose days
end without hope.
In My Human Weakness
O my God, I want to love you above all things
with my whole heart and soul,
because you are all-good and worthy of love.
But in my human weakness
I often put someone or something ahead of you.

I love my neighbor as myself
for the love of you.
But my love is imperfect,
it often falters and fails

I forgive all those who have injured me
and I ask pardon of all whom I have injured.
But, unlike You,
my forgiveness
has limits
and my pardon is slow to come.

O most holy heart of Jesus,
fountain of every blessing,
I adore you, I love you,

and with lively sorrow for my sins
I offer you this poor heart of mine.

Grant, good Jesus, that I may live
in you and for you.
Protect me in the midst of danger.
Comfort me in my afflictions.
Give me health of body,
assistance in my temporal needs,
your blessing on all that I do,
and the grace of a holy death.
Most of all, help me
suppress those unhealthy desires
that keep me from becoming
one with You.
Show Me the Way
Lord God, I give You permission to be
the Lord of my life
and the Lord of my ministry.
You, Lord, are the creator
and sustainer of the universe,
yet You have no power
over my life unless
I allow You to help me.
You are all powerful
and yet You are a
God of poverty
out of respect for my free will.
You give me, a weak pauper,
the power to say yes or no
to the abundance of grace
You wish to shower on me
every moment of my life.

Every day, in countless small ways,
I mount the throne of my life and

make myself the Lord of my life.
I say You are Lord,
but I do not relinquish my throne.
I do things my way.
Your way is often an untaken path.

You want to be the Lord of my life.
Not because You like being Lord,
or need or want to be Lord.
You want to be the Lord of my life
because You know that is
what is best for me.
And because You love me
You only want what is best for me.

O my God, I am tired of being
lord of my life.
My way is a dead end.
Your way leads to eternal life.
O my God, I give You permission
to be the Lord of my life.
Show me the way.
Amen.

Gerry on Gerry

At 68, an age when most people are comfortably settling into a life of retirement, I did something really crazy, something that took more energy and hard work than anything I had done in my life: I opened an orphanage in Port-au-Prince, Haiti, a place where hunger, violence, murder, and kidnapping were part of daily life. Seven years later, after providing some 200 abandoned kids permanent or temporary housing, food, schooling, and medical care, I'm taking on another crazy project while still operating the orphanage: publishing books. You're reading the first one. Next up is book that has been percolating within me for more than a dozen years: *Reading Thomas Merton and Longing for God in Haiti: Learning Wisdom in the School of My Life.* I consider it to be the crown jewel of my writing life.

Mine has been an unusual, even unique, journey through the turbulence of life. Nothing in my first dozen years of existence gave any indication I would be a network television producer, a documentary film director, the author of eight books, and the founder of an orphanage in the poorest country in the western hemisphere. As a child I was all but invisible. I loved being an altar boy and was lousy at all sports. My only dream (besides playing second base for the N.Y. Yankees) was to be a missionary priest in China. I tried to make the dream a reality by entering a minor seminary when I was 13 years old. I didn't last long at the seminary as the dream quickly died at the hands of doubt and confusion . . . plus failing religion and Latin didn't help inspire hope for a priestly vocation. I barely got out of high school, graduating near the very bottom of my class. I was destined to go nowhere. If someone told my family on the day of my high school graduation that one day I would work with major Hollywood stars, write books, and visit at least a dozen of the poorest nations on earth, they would have fallen down from laughter. Yet the *New York Times*, the *Los Angeles Times*, and PBS all profiled my transition from show biz to dire poverty in the worst slums on earth.

It all began with a stroke of luck in the summer of 1964 in the form of a part-time job at CBS in New York, in the audience services department. My four-week job was to respond to the huge sacks of requests for tickets to the *Ed Sullivan Show* featuring an appearance by The Beatles. I parlayed the temp job into a full-time position as a lowly clerk in the network operations division. By the time I was 35, after a series of highly unpredictable and serendipitous events, I was the associate producer of the most popular soap opera on the air, ABC's *General Hospital*, back in the "Luke & Laura on the run" days, which featured the legendary film star Elizabeth Taylor. I went on to become the supervising producer of the CBS's *Capitol*, and the executive producer of NBC's *The Doctors*, featuring a young Alec Baldwin. Those first two shows were produced in Hollywood. On that last show, I had a huge corner office at Rockefeller Center (in the heart of Manhattan) with a spectacular view of the famous ice-skating rink. Along the way, I lost my faith and considered myself an atheist.

After all the show biz fame and fortune, I was depressed and deeply unhappy . . . a lost soul longing for some deeper meaning to life. In a fleeting mystical moment of epiphany in an empty church in Rome my life completely changed. God became a reality, and his humble servant St. Francis of Assisi became God's emissary to me. I followed Francis who followed Jesus more closely than anyone ever had before him. Francis led me back to Christ and into solidarity with the poor, those living on the periphery of life, crippled by overwhelming need.

I picked up a pen and wrote about Francis. I picked up a camera and filmed the extremely poor people Christ loves and Francis would have served. When I stopped living for myself and began living for others, my life suddenly became full, rich, and rewarding...even though in Haiti I live without hot water and air conditioning and with mice and rats. In between filming in slums in Africa and South America, I gave over 250 talks at churches and university all across America and in Europe. I also taught a course on writing at the most prestigious university in the Catholic world—the Pontifical Gregorian University in Rome; more than 20 alumni of the school are canonized saints. During my first week of teaching, I sent my nephew a postcard saying: "My first day at college and I am the professor."

All of this was brilliantly captured in Joe Heil's beautifully written essay that began this book. If you skipped it, as I probably would have, then please go back to the beginning and read it. It is a story of on-going transformation that illustrates that the change you want and might need is within you. If a knucklehead such as me can change, you too can change.

My TV work was frivolous in the extreme. The shows I produced were little more than shameless vehicles to carry commercial messages to get you to buy what you do not need. Television has become a weapon of mass distraction, averting our attention from the unnecessary suffering caused by unjust poverty, and, often racism. Anyone who enters the world of extreme poverty will undergo a profound change in their worldview. I do not see myself as exceptional or special. I'm not heroic and far from being a saint. I'm just doing what I feel compelled to do. By living my faith, I'm still discovering the original goodness God planted in my being and in all humans, no matter their race or religion or sexual orientation. I've embraced the little boy who wanted to be a priest. Feeding a hungry child has become a sacramental act.

The thoughts in this book were birthed in a world of overwhelming want. My prayer is that those humble thoughts inspire you to go deeper into yourself, embrace your own goodness, and share that goodness with those in profound need in your neighborhood through your loving touch. In doing so, you are participating in the mystery of love-becoming flesh. As you bless others, you will be blessed even more.

Pax et Bonum
COMMUNICATIONS

*"Every act of mercy and kindness
brings us closer to the reality God."*

Pax et Bonum Communications is a nonprofit charitable organization whose primary purpose is to proclaim through image and word that care for the chronically poor is an essential component of the spiritual life, especially for the followers of Christ. Rooted in Franciscan spiritually, along with the mystical traditions of all faiths, *Pax et Bonum Communications* produces films and books that foster compassion for those who suffer from hunger and injustice while also inspiring genuine and respectful fraternity among all people, no matter one's faith or lack of faith.

Pax et Bonum Communications champions the importance of contemplation and action. In addition to our films, we offer free educational presentations to churches and schools that focus on two major themes: poverty and prayer. No matter our faith, we believe the best way to love God is through acts of love, mercy, compassion and kindness for those who are suffering in cruel prisons of unjust poverty. We believe everyone is called to a life of sharing, caring and giving. We believe in the importance of genuine inter-faith dialogue. We believe violence is always wrong, that war is never a solution. Our goal is to stress the necessity of prayer, peace, harmony, humility and social justice. In the spirit of St. Francis of Assisi, we hope to show the connectedness of all of creation, which will promote a deeper understanding and appreciation of the common good and our essential need to become nurturers, healers and consolers. We will not shy away from confronting the injustice of global poverty where more than

10,000 children a day die of starvation; we will be a strong, consistent and prophetic voice speaking out on behalf of the poor and encouraging people to enter more deeply into prayer and to be more compassionate to those in dire need. In that spirit we operate a home for 70 abandoned kids in Haiti.

Our name comes from the salutation always used by St. Francis: peace and good. Pax et Bonum is the Latin translation of the saint's wish for everyone he encountered. In his native Italian, Francis would have said, "pace e bene" . . . which we prefer to translate as "peace and blessing." And peace and blessing are what we hope and pray Pax et Bonum Communications offers to a world sorely in need of peace and blessing.

Pax et Bonum Communications, Inc.
Post Office Box 970
Ft. Pierce, FL 34954

Please visit our website: www.paxetbonumcomm.org

501(c)3 Public Charity • Federal Tax ID: 90-0654928